AMERICA AND THE ART
OF THE POSSIBLE

AMERICA

AND THE ART OF THE

POSSIBLE

RESTORING NATIONAL VITALITY
IN AN AGE OF DECAY

———————

CHRISTOPHER BUSKIRK

ENCOUNTER BOOKS NEW YORK · LONDON

é

First American edition published in 2023 by Encounter Books, an activity of Encounter for Culture and Education, Inc., a nonprofit, tax-exempt corporation. Encounter Books website address: www.encounterbooks.com

Manufactured in the United States and printed on acid-free paper. The paper used in this publication meets the minimum requirements of ANSI/NISO Z39.48–1992 (R 1997) (*Permanence of Paper*).

FIRST AMERICAN EDITION

LIBRARY OF CONGRESS CATALOGING-IN-PUBLICATION DATA

Names: Buskirk, Chris, 1969– author.
Title: America and the art of the possible : restoring national vitality in an age of decay / Christopher Buskirk.
Description: First American edition. | New York, New York : Encounter Books, 2023. | Includes bibliographical references and index.
Identifiers: LCCN 2021002656 (print) | LCCN 2021002657 (ebook) | ISBN 9781641771740 (hardcover) | ISBN 9781641771757 (ebook)
Subjects: LCSH: Economic development—United States—History. | Economic development—Sociological aspects. | Income distribution—United States—History. | Elite (Social sciences)—United States. | American Dream. | United States—Economic conditions—1945–
Classification: LCC HC106.5 .B86 2021 (print) | LCC HC106.5 (ebook) | DDC 330.973—DC23
LC record available at https://lccn.loc.gov/2021002656
LC ebook record available at https://lccn.loc.gov/2021002657

1 2 3 4 5 6 7 8 9 20 22

*This book is for Gina, my wife, the one I love,
who makes me and my life better...always better;
for my children, who I pray will build upon what we've
accomplished and will live their lives serving the Lord;
and for the glory of Christ the King.*

CONTENTS

INTRODUCTION

WHAT HAPPENS WHEN PROGRESS STOPS? THAT'S AN IMPORTANT question in a country whose self-understanding is deeply tied to the idea of progress—material, technological, political, and social. America's first three centuries were characterized by physically pushing our border across the continent, west to the Pacific and then across nearly 2,500 miles of open ocean. It would not have been obvious to early Americans that Hawaii, a tropical archipelago far away from the California coast, would become the nation's fiftieth state, joined in a political union with the far distant original states facing the Atlantic. At the same time the country was expanding in size, rapid progress was made in many other areas: science and technology extended the average life span, elevated living standards, and promoted social mobility and broad-based prosperity. Americans have come to expect the upward movement to continue: GDP will keep rising and science will make us healthier and wealthier, while political and cultural movements will make us better, happier people.

But progress has slowed or stalled or even reversed on various fronts in recent decades. Technology is still advancing, but primarily in the digital world. People get married later and have fewer children; life span stopped increasing and has actually declined in the past several years, even before the onset of Covid-19. It now takes two incomes to support a family of four in the middle class, whereas one income was sufficient as recently as the 1980s. Self-reported levels of happiness have dropped. Social trust is diminishing and the social consensus is badly frayed. Distrust of gatekeepers is widespread. The institutions responsible for protecting and advancing the interests of the nation—political, cultural, academic—have failed in their core mission and have become self-interested to the point of being sociopathic. In short, America has not been moving in an upward trajectory.

The uncomfortable fact is that civilizational progress doesn't happen by a law of nature and is not guaranteed to continue indefinitely. Civilizations can rise, achieve greatness, and then fade, leaving behind evidence of impressive ingenuity. For example, the Antikythera mechanism, made two thousand years ago, has been described as the first analogue computer. It's a sophisticated device for astronomical calculation found in fragmentary form near the Greek island after which it is named. The Lycurgus cup, a Roman glass goblet from the fourth century, long mystified viewers with the way it changes color from pale, opaque green to bright, translucent red when it is lit from behind. The secret was revealed by electron microscopy in 1990, showing nanoparticles of silver and gold in the glass. The effect was reproduced first by traditional glassmakers and then with a 3D printer by Dutch researchers who published their method in 2019.

To the modern mind, it is disorienting to realize that earlier civilizations could have been just as prosperous, secure, and happy as our own and perhaps more so. But the trajectory of civilization is not constantly upward. Decline and decay are just as possible as progress. In fact, decay is the default: it's what happens when you just do nothing. Samuel Huntington argued that every nation is in either a state of development or decline. This follows the classic understanding of national cycles. I would offer a modification that gets to the heart of the matter: there is an invisible force that drives development, which I call vitality.

The vitality of a nation can be judged in two ways: by the private life of its people and by the public life of the nation. In the private sphere, a nation is successful if the people are physically secure in their lives and their property; if families are being formed and are free, generally prosperous, and self-sustaining; and if those families produce at least enough children to maintain a stable population. That sounds simple, because it describes the basic conditions for personal independence, physical security, social continuity, and a general sense of well-being. Add to this a broadly accepted worldview supported by religious piety and practice and one has the conditions for a vital civilization. Rome and Athens had this. America used to have it too.

In the public sphere, civilizational vitality is shown in a capacity for collective action, which is rooted in what the fourteenth-century Arab philosopher Ibn Khaldun called *asabiyya*. This concept can be understood as social cohesion, national or civilizational purpose, a feeling of being in it together and for the same reasons. When *asabiyya* is high, societies are not just secure, they grow prosperous because high social trust supports complex trade relationships along with specialization and division of labor, allowing capacity for innovation and the production of luxury goods. Low-trust societies, in contrast, tend to have less specialization.

Just as personal vitality grows from a strong sense of identity and purpose, civilizational vitality springs from a shared identity that unites people, legitimizes the state and explains its place in the world, and inspires great societal achievements. America has undertaken big projects in the past, from taming the frontier to the early space program, but our ability to accomplish great things as a nation has waned in recent decades. One reason is a fading sense of national identity and purpose.

America's national identity was shaped in large part by the frontier and the long push westward across a continent. When the frontier closed, that aspect of the American character was set, and the nation's restless energy then went out into a global project—which has now largely run its course. Will the engine that propelled this country simply burn out? The past few decades in America have been characterized by five major themes: globalization, financialization of the economy, science and tech stagnation (despite advances in digital technology), managerialism, and risk aversion. The development of those themes has brought us to a crossroads.

Numerous indicators of societal health have been trending downward, often reinforcing each other. Some trends owe to factors outside our control, others resulted in part from earlier decisions that were made in good faith and would understandably have seemed right to most smart, informed, well-intentioned people at the time. Now it's time to reckon with those errors and correct our course. There are actions we can take that will make a difference—not silver bullets, but steps in the right direction to change our trajectory and provide a foundation for a better future.

The earlier history of the United States shows dynamism and growth on many fronts that was materially different from what we've experienced recently. In 1800 there were sixteen states with a combined population of 5.3 million. The largest city was New York, with 60,000 citizens. By 1900 the national population had grown to 73.2 million, and New York City alone counted 3.4 million people. There were forty-five states extending all the way to the Pacific. The first transcontinental railroad had been completed three decades earlier when Leland Stanford drove the golden Last Spike at Promontory Summit in Utah, uniting the nation from coast to coast.

In 1900, Stanford University was only fifteen years old but on the way to becoming one of the world's top academic institutions and an educator of American leaders. Herbert Hoover graduated from Stanford in 1895. Several other world-class universities had also been founded within a few decades beginning in 1861: the Massachusetts Institute of Technology, the first University of California campus at Berkeley, Johns Hopkins University, the University of California at Los Angeles, the University of Chicago, the California Institute of Technology, and Carnegie Mellon University.

The latter was a philanthropic project of Andrew Carnegie, who had grown fabulously wealthy from the enterprise that would become U.S. Steel in 1901. His essay titled "The Gospel of Wealth," published in 1889, was not a guide to getting rich or an early expression of Gordon Gekko's "greed is good" philosophy, but rather was about the obligation of the rich to use their wealth for the benefit of the society. It was the founding document of American philanthropy. Carnegie's own philanthropy also funded Carnegie Hall in New York, the Carnegie Endowment for International Peace, and 1,687 public libraries in the United Sates plus several hundred more around the world.

The growth kept rolling throughout most of the twentieth century. The American oil industry, led by John D. Rockefeller's Standard Oil, was already growing at a breakneck pace when Henry Ford began mass production of the automobile with his assembly line in 1913. Inventions by Thomas Edison and Nikola Tesla brought electric power to industries and households across America. Scientific advances—some beginning in the United States, some in other countries—were a key driver of improvements in living standards.

The early twentieth century was a golden age of physics, bringing the discovery of the electron and the photon, Einstein's general theory of relativity, and a fuller understanding of quantum mechanics. New knowledge in physics led to previously impossible practical applications. One of the most important was the development of the transistor at Bell Laboratories in 1947, providing a more compact replacement for the vacuum tube as a logic component in computers. Vacuum tubes are large and heavy, which made powerful computers prohibitively large before an alternative was developed. Transistors are small and have been shrinking for decades: an iPhone 13 contains fifteen billion of them. A huge leap forward in physics—the world of atoms—inaugurated the information age.

Highly consequential advances were occurring in medicine too. One of the greatest was the understanding of antibiotics, and particularly the discovery of penicillin by Alexander Fleming in 1928, which followed a syphilis treatment discovered in 1909. Fleming was a Scot, and though British researchers began working toward large-scale manufacture, it was an American company, Pfizer, that developed the process of deep tank fermentation, enabling mass production just in time to provide penicillin to the troops making the D-Day landing. More than half of the antibiotics used today were discovered between 1937 and 1971. Today there are no antibiotics made in the United States, which indicates not just stagnation in basic science, but a degradation of manufacturing capacity.

Many one-time-only advances were made in that earlier era: discovering electricity, curing polio, developing antibiotics. These singular advances brought great material improvements to people's lives, and the benefits were widely distributed. Let's look at the average American home in 1900: by the best estimate, only 1 percent of homes had indoor plumbing.[1] There was no electric light, no refrigerator, no telephone, no washing machine, no television, no car parked outside. All of these things were standard in the average American home by 1960. The typical home of 2022 wouldn't look greatly different: the TV is probably a large flat-screen with many more channels; there are multiple phones and maybe no land line; there's a PC or some laptops and tablets with internet. But the differences aren't as dramatic as those between 1900 and 1960.

Things were changing fast and for the better before 1960. America was growing, people were living longer and healthier lives, and living standards were rising. There was a lot of momentum behind American expansion, and when progress slowed down it wasn't really noticeable for a while. But science has been advancing more slowly and at greater cost, resulting in slower development of new technology that improves living standards, a slower increase in productivity, and lower real economic growth.

This is what Tyler Cowen called "the Great Stagnation" in a book with that title, published in 2010. A decade later, few people seem willing to accept the idea. Acknowledging that we're in a period of stagnation seems like a form of heresy, even if the effects are all around us: stagnant wages, a widening wealth gap, a shrinking middle class, endless cycles of debt that trap people in what David Graeber called bullshit jobs, which he defined as "a form of paid employment that is so completely pointless, unnecessary, or pernicious that even the employee cannot justify its existence even though, as part of the conditions of employment, the employee feels obliged to pretend that this is not the case." Obesity and chronic inflammatory diseases have become more widespread. Loneliness and alienation have been rising since before Robert Putnam wrote *Bowling Alone* in 2000. Social cohesion is weaker and political polarization is sharper. Americans even stopped having enough children to keep the population steady, let alone expand it. One consequence of low birth rates is that the median age of Americans has climbed from 28.1 in 1970 to 38.3 in 2020 as the younger generations have gotten relatively smaller. As American society has grown older, it has also become more risk-averse, less willing to take on big challenges that could lead to a more prosperous future.

The main consequence of stagnation is a loss of social mobility. The promise of modern American liberalism is that if you work hard and play by the rules, you will do better than your parents, and if you go to college, a secure place in the middle class should be a near certainty. Yet it has become harder for people to get ahead, and many find themselves running just to stand still. Now, each new generation is doing worse than the one before it. At every stage of life, Generation X has owned a smaller share of the national wealth than Baby Boomers did at the same median age, while Millennials own even less.

It's easy to see why Millennials are sometimess characterized as the Lost Generation and why sociopathologies—including high rates of drug use, sexual dysfunction, depression, and other mental health issues—are so much in evidence among them, along with radical politics. They are a large part of American society, but because they hold such a small share of national wealth relative to the preceding generations at their age, they are more alienated from the system and resentful of the status quo. As a result, they look for answers. They're not just asking "Why are things the way they are?" but "I'm an adult now, how do I get my rightful share?" Since the political mainstream appears to have failed them, many are inclined to seek answers outside it. One way to understand the rise of Bitcoin is as an end-run around the existing financial system, which remains disproportionately controlled by Boomers. The Millennials and Zoomers who see little hope for success within it are building an alternative.

We're seeing a pattern of downward mobility and a proletarianization of the American people. There are declining prospects for individuals, increasing precarity, and more social dysfunction. There is more inequality and more polarization, both contributing to institutional decay. These symptoms have been much remarked upon, but the underlying malady has gone undiagnosed. If we want to arrest the disintegrative trends, we need to start by recognizing that the decay is further advanced and far deeper than either the Left or the Right will admit. It also cuts across the left/right political dialectic that has prevailed since the end of World War II.

As much as these things are discussed, the causes are often misunderstood. Adding to the slowdown in science, there are structural demographic forces that combined to create an environment ripe for conflict. The symptoms of societal decay are typically seen through a narrowly ideological lens. Political liberals blame billionaires, greed and bigotry for growing inequality, and call for redistributing wealth from billionaires to everyone else—which would not solve the underlying problem. Some conservatives see insufficient devotion to the cause of liberty behind the country's malaise, while others identify a spiritual crisis leading to cultural degradation. While I'm quite sympathetic to the idea that there is a spiritual deficit in America, it is only part of the problem I'm describing here.

What is usually missed in efforts to diagnose the problem is the lack of real economic growth. The abundance that comes from growth is a basis of social and political stability in the United States. It's not the only one, but it has been central to American expectations from the beginning. The promise of growth is built into the social fabric and central to decisions we make individually and as a nation. Americans are forming long-term plans, like what career to pursue and how to invest for retirement, on the assumption that the sustained growth that occurred between the late eighteenth century and roughly 1970 is still ongoing. But it isn't. Government has made commitments based on the same false premise, and it cannot fulfill them. State and local pension plans have promised benefits to retirees that require average annual returns of 7 percent to 10 percent on their investment portfolio, but many don't achieve those returns over the long term. Managers resort to financial gimmicks to paper over the problem, hoping that future returns will get them back to even. The problems with solvency in Social Security and Medicare are well known but consistently ignored.

We expect the American economy to achieve sustained real growth of something like 3 percent annually, but it has been very low, perhaps 1 percent, for a long time. And there is currently no obvious path to sustained real growth of 2 percent or higher. Short-term policy tricks have masked the problem and created false confidence, while also incentivizing malinvestment. Many conservatives have grown intellectually lazy and addicted to preaching supply-side tax cuts as the path out of the growth desert. The Laffer curve, created in 1974 to represent the economic and fiscal benefits of lower taxes, is blindly accepted as true for all times and places. It appeared true enough during the Reagan years, when marginal tax rates had been quite high before the reductions, but we've reached the point of greatly diminishing returns at best, and the true believers have become a cargo cult. Reducing the top marginal tax rate from 37 percent to 33 percent might be a good thing, but it's not going to catalyze another great era of growth like the one in the early twentieth century.

Real economic growth is achieved by increasing either population or productivity. Americans don't give birth to enough children to maintain the current population. Even if we did, we would still need the sort of economic growth that comes from higher productivity, which results primarily from technological advances that increase output per unit of input. Slow or no population growth married to slow or no productivity growth in a society with embedded obligations premised upon growth will lead into a Malthusian trap that can be dangerously destabilizing.

In addition to slow population growth, innovation has also slowed down in the past several decades, for reasons that are not fully understood. Did we already eat all the low-hanging fruit? Have we reached a Pareto limit of what can be known about the natural world? Are we too risk-averse? Are original ideas stifled by pressure to conform to fashionable dogmas that shuts out the unique, heterodox minds that often push science forward? Are institutional incentives misdirected? The answer is probably all of them in some measure. What's usually overlooked is a slowdown in scientific discovery. We believe that science is advancing rapidly, but scientists have been stuck on some intractable problems for a long time. Cancer remains uncured, nuclear fusion remains elusive, and we famously got Twitter instead of the flying cars we were promised.

Are there presently reasons for hope? Yes. There is promise in some areas, such as new medical therapies and advances in energy technologies, but they seem unlikely to be realized in a way that decisively changes our trajectory and fuels robust, long-term productivity growth anytime soon.

Many of the problems facing America today can be seen throughout the developed world, but the solutions will need to be distinctly American. A prerequisite for recovering national vitality is to regain a national purpose and identity. In this age of heightened awareness of group identities, the national identity that binds us together is given short shrift when the very concept isn't being decried as oppressive. When a people loses its sense of itself and its place and purpose in the world, it disintegrates from within.

Any nation's self-conception is rooted in its particular history and place. America was a frontier nation from the landing at Jamestown in 1607 onward. Americans were settlers and builders, pushing across a continent and creating a new nation out of nothing. The wide frontier and the abundant available land gave Americans a sense of agency and possibility. That land also acted as a sort of economic subsidy: it was free raw material waiting to be combined with intelligence, energy, and effort. The frontier also provided a national purpose: get to the Pacific and populate everything in between. Everyone could participate somehow, even those who stayed behind. Maybe they didn't pound spikes for the railroad but they might have produced the steel that made it possible.

It's hard to overstate the importance of the frontier in forming the character of the American nation. It is on frontiers that innovation happens, ideas are put to the test, and the capacity for collective action is developed. Why? Because it must. Frontiers are the ultimate stressor: it's always do or die.

Another aspect of America's historic national identity, derived from its European cultural heritage, came to be highly contested. The settling of the frontier occurred within the context of a spiritual contest for the soul of the nation. Is America a nation defined by the Christian tradition brought from Europe, as was believed by the earliest settlers and by most Americans through much of the nineteenth century? Or is it a creation of secular Enlightenment philosophy, couched at first in the language of Christianity but essentially in tension with it? Could those two national self-conceptions coexist? These questions continue to animate American politics, but the contest was muted when the national identity was centered on expanding across a continent.

When the western frontier was closed by the Pacific Ocean, there was still a lot of building to be done. The Pacific coastal states were all added by 1889, but several territories in the interior were yet to gain statehood, the last being New Mexico and Arizona in 1912. Alaska and Hawaii were still to come, of course, but meanwhile the world wars intervened and consumed much of the restless energy of the still young, still vital nation as we turned our attentions abroad.

The United States was a latecomer to the Great Game era of colonialism. Americans had been busy claiming a continent, and foreign policy had largely been governed by the principles that George Washington set forth in his Farewell Address. In that speech—even a single reading of which demonstrates why Washington was the indispensable American—he urged Americans to pursue an independent destiny, at peace with the world as far as it was within our power, serene within our borders, protected by a wide ocean on one side and a broad, untamed continent on the other. It would only be to our detriment to become entangled in the rivalries and enmities of foreign powers. Washington said:

The great rule of conduct for us, in regard to foreign nations, is, in extending our commercial relations, to have with them as little political connexion as possible. So far as we have already formed engagements, let them be fulfilled with perfect good faith. Here let us stop.

Europe has a set of primary interests, which to us have none, or a very remote relation. Hence she must be engaged in frequent controversies, the causes of which are essentially foreign to our concerns. Hence, therefore, it must be unwise in us to implicate ourselves, by artificial ties, in the ordinary vicissitudes of her politics, or the ordinary combinations and collisions of her friendships or enmities.

Our detached and distant situation invites and enables us to pursue a different course.

An attitude of benign neutrality was at the heart of American foreign policy until the early twentieth century because it was part of the national self-conception. Americans saw themselves as having an independent destiny.

But that changed with World War I, when the United States inserted itself into a European war and tipped the balance. This was done by design. The Progressives of the time saw it as a way of gaining a role in Great Power diplomacy. Teddy Roosevelt's Great White Fleet steaming around the world was impressive but insufficient. The decisive use of American might in war is what made European powers welcome the rise of American internationalism, which in turn encouraged Progressives like Woodrow Wilson and others who saw America as a messianic power in the world. Americans were told that the Great War was fought "to make the world safe for democracy."

World War I occurred just as several secular trends were peaking. In particular, the war was effectively the coda for the first modern period of globalization. It was also a time of rapid innovation and productivity growth. Americans had a new sense of the country's industrial might and of the martial power that came with it. That led to a reconception of America's role in the world and the national identity. The change that began in 1917 was consummated in 1945, when victory in World War II put the United States in a position to remake the world order. The energy that had been focused on taming the frontier was transferred seamlessly into that new project.

In an underappreciated twist, America and the Soviet Union were engaged in a similar project throughout the Cold War: an effort to replace the old colonial order with a new order led by themselves. The Soviets backed Marxist revolutionaries fighting to oust European colonial powers in the hope of replacing them with client regimes. Likewise, the United States encouraged decolonization and backed anticommunist insurgents around the world. The goal was the same: to cultivate client states through which we would refashion the world in our own image. This was the Great Game 2.0 and it became the main American project of the post–World War II era.

Globalization, envisioned as a world order with America at its head, has been the central project of the United States since the end of World War II. It has been the means by which we created an empire and enforced our imperial will. Western European nations, exhausted from two world wars and then facing a cold war, came along for the ride. Officially, they were junior partners, but in practice they were well-paid vassals. Some good came out of the American postwar policy, but also a raft of unintended consequences, as is normal in a complex, imperfect world. There were decisions made in the context of the Cold War that worked relatively well for the purposes of the time, but had some negative results in the long run.

Part of the American project was dollar supremacy. As World War II was drawing to a close, the United States entered into the Bretton Woods Agreement with its allies, which established that the dollar would be the reserve currency of the war's winners and that it would be convertible into gold. The second element is gone, but the first one still holds. Dollar supremacy gave the United States a unique advantage over other countries, and it gave politicians tremendous power at home, allowing them to run massive deficits year upon year and accumulate a national debt that now exceeds GDP without causing broad consumer inflation. We don't yet know how far we can stretch the limits of the power the United States draws from possessing a fiat currency that is also the world's reserve currency, in combination with political and military hegemony. Finding those limits is likely to be painful.

Dollar supremacy is similar to the "resource curse" in countries rich in natural resources. The concept, once called the Dutch disease, refers to the paradox that some countries, finding themselves blessed with an abundance of a valuable commodity—such as oil in Saudi Arabia and Venezuela, or diamonds in the Democratic Republic of the Congo— come to rely so heavily on the easy money it brings that they fail to develop a broad-based economy or supporting social institutions. America's resource is dollars made valuable by military and economic power and political stability. And we have an infinite supply of them. But as in other resource-dependent countries, the easy money is a trap. It leads to malinvestment and then to recurring economic crises, which are answered by ever larger monetary and fiscal interventions. When Saudi Arabia or Russia has an economic problem, it pumps more oil. When America has a problem, we print more dollars.

Fiat currency has allowed Americans to create an economy based on debt, and not just government debt. A lot of ink has been spilled on the problem of deficits and debt, and the virtue of sound money and fiscal probity. But it's no coincidence that the era of debt in America (discussed more in Chapter 1) is also a time of slowing innovation and growth. Those things are intertwined: Fiscal solutions are used to cover up deeper problems in the economy, but they also prolong those problems by creating more incentives for malinvestment.

Another postwar policy that made sense at the time of implementation was eliminating trade restrictions in the belief that deeper trading relationships would build a tighter alliance against the international communism being exported by the Soviet Union. There was certainly truth in that theory. But there were also costs that exploded after the collapse of the Soviet Union, when so-called free trade was most aggressively pursued. I say "so-called" because the free-trade agreements are complicated, heavily negotiated legal agreements that provide advantages and disadvantages to favored or forgotten industries. In the 1970s and 1980s, American manufacturing came under growing pressure from Asian competition, which intensified in the 1990s and 2000s, especially after China was admitted to the Word Trade Organization in 2001.

For a time, globalization primarily affected unskilled workers, as their jobs were automated, exported to China, or given to off-the-books illegal labor. But the effects expanded into the middle class, as manufacturing and supporting jobs were shipped overseas. In the past decade, even professional and managerial jobs—the province of the upper middle class—have been threatened by globalization. This is not an indictment of the people who saw benefits in promoting freer trade, but of the complacent class who have allowed the outdated solutions to yesterday's problems to kill the prospects for a prosperous tomorrow.

What was unquestionably good about the postwar policy is that it was a national project, with a role for nearly everyone to play, just as there had been during our frontier era. That project was global and had political, military, economic, and cultural facets. American companies sold products like Coke, Levi's, and Marlboros all around the world, and built fast food restaurants on the Champs-Élysées (a tragedy). Hollywood came to dominate movies and television worldwide, first showcasing American strength, then broadcasting decadence. Wall Street became the center of global finance, and Silicon Valley the epicenter of tech innovation. In some ways they were at odds—while Silicon Valley was innovating, Wall Street starting in the 1980s was leading the charge to financialize the economy. American farming was remade in the early 1970s by the secretary of agriculture, Earl Butts, into the industrial, monocultural corporate enterprise that it is today. American agricultural exports boomed.

Now the American hyperproject has run its course. The factories have been exported, and proletarianization is trickling up from the American working class to the professional managerial class. Even the merely rich are being left behind by the superrich. Industrial agriculture has exacted a great cost on the family farm and the environment. American pop culture, while still a powerful global phenomenon, is increasingly rejected by people in central and eastern Europe, across Asia, in the Indian subcontinent, and elsewhere in favor of homegrown culture that better reflects local sensibilities. Since 1941, the American military has never been completely at peace. After World War II came the Cold War and interventions in Korea, Vietnam, Africa, Colombia, Nicaragua, Grenada, Iraq, Kuwait, Bosnia, Somalia, Iraq again, Afghanistan, Syria, Yemen, and so on. Our military interventions have become a tragic farce that undermines our security, bleeds our young people, and distracts attention from problems at home. The Great Power competition of the nineteenth century gave way to the ideological conflict of the twentieth century and is now being replaced by rivalries between civilization-states, particularly China, India, and Russia.

These are big changes in the way the world works, yet American elites still cling to a worldview born in the 1940s. It's past time to rethink the national project and identity, and then move forward boldly.

One prerequisite for moving in a positive direction is to recognize the value of accepting risk. That may seem counterintuitive when any number of studies demonstrate that most people will choose security over freedom, justice, equality, or almost anything else. In fact, it's difficult to accomplish normal things like raising a family when you have too much risk in your life, especially the wrong types of risk. There's a big difference between the risk of taking Oxycontin and that of starting a homestead on the edge of civilization.

Mitigating risk has always been a central concern of human societies and a reason for individuals to band together in the first place. Modern societies, especially in the West, have been very successful in reducing many of the risks that historically brought much misery and death. Few people in modern societies are at risk of death by starvation. Childhood mortality has dropped so precipitously that the death of a child is considered a rare tragedy rather than a grim commonplace. Medications reduce the duration and intensity of many illnesses that were once so crippling and deadly. There have been wars aplenty in the modern world, but America is not at risk of a military invasion. We sit secure between two oceans, dominant in our hemisphere, even if we choose not to control our own borders.

The mitigation of risk is generally beneficial, but it also breeds complacency and a reluctance to take on big challenges that can move us forward. Looking back at the successes of the past several generations, it's too easy to assume that progress is simply natural, when in fact it results from bold and courageous action.

Taking risks was a defining part of the American culture from the time the Pilgrims crossed an ocean to settle in a strange land, through the era of pioneers in covered wagons venturing into the wilderness, and to the day that astronauts landed on the moon. Ironically, our society's present risk aversion puts us in a very risky situation because it has caused stagnation, which increases social dysfunction and political conflict, and makes us less equipped to meet emerging global challenges. We need to recognize the danger we are in and be willing to take on risks to reverse the forces of decay. We can all have a part in restoring the national vitality that benefits all Americans.

1

AN AGE OF DECAY

AMERICA RAN OUT OF FRONTIER WHEN WE HIT THE PACIFIC Ocean. And that changed things. Alaska and Hawaii were too far away to figure in most people's aspiration, so for decades it was the West Coast states and especially California that represented dreams and possibilities in the national imagination. The American dream reached its apotheosis in California. After World War II, the state became our collective tomorrow. But today it looks more like a future that the rest of the country should avoid—a place where a few coastal enclaves have grown fabulously wealthy while everyone else falls further and further behind.

After World War II, California led the way on every front. The population was growing quickly as people moved to the state in search of opportunity and young families had children. The economy was vibrant and diverse. Southern California benefited from the presence of defense contractors. San Diego was a Navy town, and demobilized GIs returning from the Pacific Front decided to stay and put down roots. Between 1950 and 1960, the population of the Los Angeles metropolitan area swelled from 4,046,000 to 6,530,000.[1] The Jet Propulsion Laboratory had been inaugurated in the 1930s by researchers at the California Institute of Technology. One of the founders, Jack Parsons, became a prominent member of an occult sect in the

I

late 1940s based in Pasadena that practiced "Thelemic Magick" in ceremonies called the "Babalon Working." L. Ron Hubbard, the founder of Scientology (1950), was an associate of Parsons and rented rooms in his home. The counterculture, or rather, counter cultures, had deep roots in the state.

Youth culture was born in California, arising out of a combination of rapid growth, the Baby Boom, the general absence of extended families, plentiful sunshine, the car culture, and the space afforded by newly built suburbs where teenagers could be relatively free from adult supervision. Tom Wolfe memorably described this era in his 1963 essay "The Kandy-Colored Tangerine Flake Streamline, Baby." The student protest movement began in California too. In 1960, hundreds of protesters, many from the University of California at Berkeley, sought to disrupt a hearing of the House Un-American Activities Committee at the San Francisco City Hall. The police turned firehoses on the crowd and arrested over thirty students. The Baby Boomers may have inherited the protest movement, but they didn't create it. Its founders were part of the Silent Generation. Clark Kerr, the president of the UC system who earned a reputation for giving student protesters what they wanted, was from the Greatest Generation. Something in California, and in America, had already changed.

California was a sea of ferment during the 1960s—a turbulent brew of contrasting trends, as Tom O'Neill described it:

> The state was the epicenter of the summer of love, but it had also seen the ascent of Reagan and Nixon. It had seen the Watts riots, the birth of the antiwar movement, and the Altamont concert disaster, the Free Speech movement and the Hells Angels. Here, defense contractors, Cold Warriors, and nascent tech companies lived just down the road from hippie communes, love-ins, and surf shops.[2]

Hollywood was the entertainment capital of the world, producing a vision of peace and prosperity that it sold to interior America—and to the world as the *beau ideal* of the American experiment. It was a prosperous life centered around the nuclear family living in a single-family home in the burgeoning suburbs. Doris Day became America's sweetheart through a series of romantic comedies, but the turbulence in her own life foreshadowed America's turn from vitality to decay. She was married three times, and her first husband either embezzled or mismanaged her substantial fortune. Her son, Terry Melcher, was closely associated with Charles Manson and the Family, along with Dennis Wilson of the Beach Boys—avatars of the California lifestyle that epitomized the American dream. The Manson Family spent the summer of 1968 living and partying with Wilson in his Malibu mansion. The Cielo Drive home in the Hollywood Hills where Sharon Tate and four others were murdered in August 1969 had been Melcher's home and the site of parties that Manson attended. The connections between Doris Day's son, the Beach Boys, and the Manson Family has a darkly prophetic valence in retrospect. They were young, good-looking, and carefree. But behind the clean-cut image of wholesome American youth was a desperate decadence fueled by titanic drug abuse, sexual outrages that were absurd even by the standards of Hollywood in the Sixties, and self-destructiveness clothed in the language of pseudo-spirituality.

The California culture of the 1960s now looks like a fin-de-siècle blow-off top. The promise, fulfillment, and destruction of the American dream appears distilled in the Golden State, like an epic tragedy played out against a sunny landscape where the frontier ended. Around 1970, America entered into an age of decay and California was in the vanguard.

The expectation of constant progress is deeply ingrained in our understanding of the world, and of America in particular. Some metrics do generally keep rising: gross domestic product mostly goes up, and so does the stock market. According to those barometers, things must be headed mostly in the right direction. Sure there are temporary setbacks—the economy has recessions, the stock market has corrections—but the long-term trajectory is upward. Are those metrics telling us that the country is growing more prosperous? Are they signal or noise?

There is much that GDP and the stock market don't tell us about, such as public and private debt levels, wage trends, and wealth concentration. In fact, during a half century in which reported GDP grew consistently and the stock market reached the stratosphere, real wages have crept up very slowly and living standards have flatlined or even declined for the middle and working classes. Many Americans have a feeling that things aren't going in the right direction or that the country has lost its societal health and vigor, but aren't sure how to describe or measure the problem. We need broader metrics of national prosperity and vitality, including measures of noneconomic values like family stability or social trust.

There are many different criteria for national vitality. First, is the country guarded against foreign aggression, and at peace with itself? Are people secure in their homes, free from government harassment and safe from violent crime? Is prosperity broadly shared? Can the average person get a good job, buy a house, and support a family without doing anything extraordinary? Are families growing? Are people generally healthy, and is life span increasing or at least not decreasing? Is social trust high? Do people have a sense of unity in a common destiny and purpose? Is there a high capacity for collective action? Are people happy?

We can sort quantifiable metrics of vitality into three main categories: social, economic, and political. There is a spiritual element too, which for my purposes falls under the social category. The social factors that can readily be measured include things like age at first marriage (an indicator of optimism about the future), median adult stature (is it rising or declining?), life expectancy, and prevalence of disease. Economic measures include real wage trends, wealth concentration, and social mobility. Political metrics relate to polarization and acts of political violence. Many of these tend to move together over long periods of time. It's easy to look at an individual metric and miss the forest for the trees, not seeing how it's one manifestation of a larger problem in a dynamic system. Solutions proposed to deal with one concern may cause unexpected new problems in another part of the system. It's a society-wide game of whack-a-mole. What's needed is a more comprehensive understanding of structural trends and what lies behind them.

From the founding period in America until about 1830, those factors were generally improving. Life expectancy and median height were increasing, both indicating a society that was mostly at peace and had plentiful food. Real wages roughly tripled during this period as labor supply growth was slow. There was some political violence, but for decades after independence the country was largely at peace and citizens were secure in their homes. There was an overarching sense of shared purpose in building a new nation.

Those indicators of vitality are no longer trending upward. Let's start with life expectancy. There is a general impression that up until the last century people died very young. There's an element of truth to this: we are now less susceptible to death from infectious disease, especially in early childhood, than were our ancestors before the twentieth century. Childhood mortality rates were appalling in the past, but burying a young child is now a rare tragedy. This is a very real form of progress, resulting from more reliable food supplies as a result of improvements in agriculture, better sanitation in cities, and medical advances, particularly the antibiotics and certain vaccines introduced in the first half of the twentieth century. A period of rapid progress was then followed by a long period of slow, expensive improvement at the margin.

When you factor out childhood mortality, life spans have not grown by much in the past century or two. A study in the *Journal of the Royal Society of Medicine* says that in mid-Victorian England, life expectancy at age five was 75 for men and 73 for women. In 2016, according to the Social Security Administration, the American male life expectancy at age five was 71.53 (which means living to age 76.53). Once you've made it to five years, your life expectancy is not much different from your great-grandfather's. Moreover, Pliny tells us that Cicero's wife Terentia lived to 103. Eleanor of Aquitaine, queen of both France and England at different times in the twelfth century, died a week shy of her 82nd birthday. A study of 298 famous men born before 100 BC who were not murdered, killed in battle, or by suicide found that their average age at death was 71.[3]

More striking is that people who live completely outside of modern civilization without Western medicine today have life expectancies rough-ly comparable to our own. Daniel Lieberman, a biological anthropologist at Harvard, notes that "foragers who survive the precarious first few years of infancy are most likely to live to be 68 to 78 years old."[4] In some ways they are healthier in old age than the average American, with lower inci-dences of inflammatory diseases like diabetes and atherosclerosis. It should be no surprise that an active life spent outside in the sun, eating wild game and foraged plants, produces good health.

Recent research shows that not only are we not living longer, we are less healthy and less mobile during the last decades of our lives than our great-grand-fathers were. This points to a *decline* in overall health. We have new drugs to treat Type I diabetes, but there is more Type I diabetes than in the past. We have new treatments for cancer, but there is more cancer. Something has gone very wrong. What's more, between 2014 and 2017, median American life ex-pectancy declined every year. In 2017 it was 78.6 years,[5] then it decreased again between 2018 and 2020, to 76.87.[6] The figure for 2020 includes Covid deaths, of course, but the trend was already heading downward for several years, most-ly from deaths of despair: diseases associated with chronic alcoholism, drug overdoses, and suicide. The reasons for the increase in deaths of despair are complex, but a major contributing factor is economic: people without good prospects over an extended period of time are more prone to self-destructive behavior. This decline is in contrast to the experience of peer countries.

In addition to life expectancy, other upward trends have stalled or reversed in the past few decades. Family formation has slowed. The total fertility rate has dropped to well below replacement level. Real wages have stagnated. Debt levels have soared. Social mobility has stalled and income inequality has grown. Material conditions for most people have improved little except in narrow parts of life such as entertainment.

The last several decades have been a story of losing ground for much of middle America, away from a handful of wealthy cities on the coasts. The optimistic story that's been told is that both income and wealth have been rising. That's true in the aggregate, but when those numbers are broken down the picture is one of a rising gap between a small group of winners and a larger group of losers. Real wages have remained essentially flat over the past fifty years, and the growth in national wealth has been heavily concentrated at the top. The chart below represents the share of national income that went to the top 10 percent of earners in the United States. In 1970 it was 33.3 percent; in 2019 the figure was 45.4 percent.[7]

FIGURE ONE

Share of National Income to Top 10 Percent of U.S. Earners

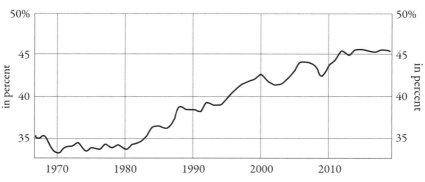

Source: World Inequality Database, "Top 10% national income share,"
https://wid.world/world/.

Disparities in wealth have become more closely tied to educational attainment. Between 1989 and 2019, household wealth grew the most for those with the highest level of education. For households with a graduate degree, the increase was 31 percent; with a college degree, it was 17 percent; with a high school degree, about 4 percent. Meanwhile, household wealth declined by a precipitous 60 percent for high school dropouts, including those with a GED. In 1989, households with a college degree had 2.74 times the wealth of those with only a high school diploma; in 2012 it was 3.08 times as much. In 1989, households with a graduate degree had 4.85 times the wealth of the high school group; in 2019 it was 6.12 times as much. The gap between the graduate degree group and the college group increased by 12 percent. The high school group's wealth grew about 4 percent from 1989 to 2019, the college group's wealth grew about 17 percent, and the wealth of the graduate degree group increased 31 percent. The gaps between the groups are growing in real dollars. It's true that people have some control over the level of education they attain, but college has become costlier and it's fundamentally unnecessary for many jobs, so the growing wealth disparity by education is a worrying trend.

Wealth is relative: if your wealth grew by 4 percent while that of another group increased by 17 percent, then you are poorer. What's more crucial, however, is purchasing power. If the costs of middle-class staples like health care, housing, and college tuition are climbing sharply while wages stagnate, then living standards will decline.

More problematic than growing wealth disparity in itself is diminishing economic mobility. A big part of the American story from the beginning has been that children tend to end up better off than their parents were. By most measures that hasn't been true for decades.

The chart below compares the birth cohorts of 1940 and 1980 in terms of earning more than parents did.[8] The horizontal axis indicates the relative income level of the parents. Among the older generation, over 90 percent earned more than their parents, except for those whose parents were at the very high end of the income scale. Among the younger generation, the percentages were much lower, and also more variable. For those whose parents had a median income, only about 40 percent would do better. In this analysis, low growth and high inequality both suppress mobility.

Over time, declining economic mobility becomes an intergenerational problem, as younger people fall behind the preceding generation in wealth accumulation. The graph below illustrates the proportion of the national wealth held by successive generations at the same stage of life, with the horizontal axis indicating median age for the group. Baby Boomers (birth years 1946–1964) owned a much larger percentage of the national wealth than the two succeeding generations at every point.

8

An Age of Decay

FIGURE TWO

*Percentage of U.S. Children Who Earn More Than
Their Parents with Simulations*

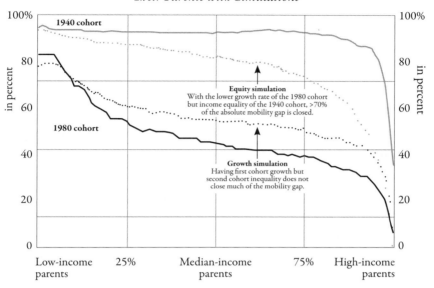

Source: Austin Clemens, "Eight graphs that tell the story of U.S. income inequality,"
Washington Center for Equitable Growth, December 9, 2019.

FIGURE THREE

Share of National Wealth Owned by Each Generation

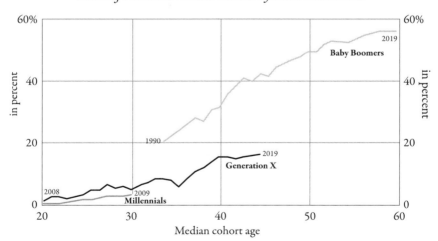

Source: Christopher Ingraham, "The staggering millennial wealth deficit, in one chart,"
Washington Post, December 3, 2019 (chart adapted from Gray Kimbrough).

9

At a median age of forty-five, for example, the Boomers owned approximately 40 percent of the national wealth. At the same median age, Generation X (1965–1980) owned about 15 percent. The Boomer generation was 15–18 percent larger than Gen X and it had 2.67 times as much of the national wealth. The Millennial generation (1981–1996) is bigger than Gen X though a little smaller than the Boomers, and it has owned about half what Gen X did at the same median age.

Those are some measurable indicators of the nation's vitality, and they tell us that something is going wrong. A key reason for stagnant wages, declining mobility, and growing disparities of wealth is that economic growth overall has been sluggish since around 1970. And the main reason for slower growth is that the long-term growth in productivity that created so much wealth for America and the world over the prior two centuries slowed down.

There are other ways to increase the overall national wealth. One is by acquiring new resources, which has been done in various ways: through territorial conquest, or the incorporation of unsettled frontier lands, or the discovery of valuable resources already in a nation's territory, such as petroleum reserves in recent history. Getting an advantageous trade agreement can also be a way of increasing resources. Through much of American history, the frontier was a great source of new wealth. The vast supply of mostly free land, along with the other resources it held, was not just an economic boon; it also shaped American culture and politics in ways that were distinct from the long-settled countries of Europe where the frontier had been closed for centuries and all the land was owned space. But there can be a downside to becoming overly dependent on any one resource.

Aside from gaining new resources, real economic growth comes from either population growth or productivity growth. Population growth can add to the national wealth, but also put strain on supplies of essential resources. What elevates living standards broadly is productivity growth, making more out of available resources. A farmer who tills his fields with a steel plough pulled by a horse can cultivate more land than a farmer doing it by hand. It allows him to produce more food that can be consumed by a bigger family, or the surplus can be sold or traded for other goods. A farmer driving a plough with an engine and reaping with a mechanical combine can produce even more. But productivity growth is driven by innovation. In the example above, there is a progression from farming by hand with a simple tool, to the use of metal tools and animal power, to the use of complicated machinery, each of which greatly increases the amount of food produced per farmer. This illustrates the basic truth that technology is a means of reducing scarcity and generating surpluses of essential goods, so labor and resources can be put toward other purposes and the whole population will be better off.

Total factor productivity (TFP) refers to economic output relative to the size of all primary inputs, namely labor and capital. Over time, a nation's economic output tends to grow faster than its labor force and capital stock. This might owe to better labor skills or capital management, but it is primarily the result of new technology. In economics, productivity growth is used as a proxy for the application of innovation. If productivity is rising, it is understood to mean that applied science is working to reduce scarcity.

The countries that lead in technological innovation naturally reap the benefits first and most broadly, and therefore have the highest living standards. Developing countries eventually get the technology too, and then enjoy the benefits in what is called catch-up growth. For example, China first began its national electrification program in the 1950s, when electricity was nearly ubiquitous in the United States. The project took a few decades to complete, and China saw rapid growth as wide access to electric power increased productivity.

The United States still leads the way in innovation—though now with more competition than at any time since World War II. But the development of productivity-enhancing new technologies has been slower over the past few decades than in any comparable span of time since the beginning of the Industrial Revolution in the early eighteenth century. The obvious advances in a few specific areas, particularly digital technology, are exceptions that prove the rule. The social technologies of recent years facilitate consumption rather than production. As a result, growth in total factor productivity has been slow for a long time. According to a report from Rabobank, "TFP growth deteriorated from an average annual growth of 1.1% over the period 1969–2010 to 0.4% in 2010 to 2018."[9]

In *The Great Stagnation*, Tyler Cowen suggested that the conventional productivity measures may be misleading. For example, he noted that productivity growth through 2000–2004 averaged 3.8 percent, a very high figure and an outlier relative to most of the last half century. Surely some of that growth was real owing to the growth of the internet at the time, but it also coincided with robust growth in the financial sector, which ended very badly in 2008. "What we measured as value creation actually may have been value destruction, namely too many homes and too much financial innovation of the wrong kind."[10] Then, productivity shot up by over 5 percent in 2009–2010, but Cohen found that it was mostly the result of firms firing the least productive people. That may have been good business, but it's not the same as productivity rising because innovation is reducing scarcity and thus leading to better living standards.

Over the long term, when productivity growth slows or stalls, overall economic growth is sluggish. Median real wage growth is slow. For most people, living standards don't just stagnate but decline.

As productivity growth has slowed, the economy has become more financialized, which means that resources are increasingly channeled into means of extracting wealth from the productive economy instead of producing goods and services. Peter Thiel said that a simple way to understand financialization is that it represents the increasing influence of companies whose main business or source of value is producing little pieces of paper that essentially say, *you owe me money*. Wall Street and the companies that make up the financial sector have never been larger or more powerful. Since the early 1970s, financial firms' share of all corporate earnings has roughly doubled, to nearly 25 percent. As a share of real GDP, it grew from 13–15 percent in the early 1970s to nearly 22 percent in 2020.[11] The profits of financial firms have grown faster than their share of the economy over the past half century.

The examples are everywhere. Many companies that were built to produce real-world, nondigital goods and services have become stealth finance companies too. General Electric, the manufacturing giant founded by Thomas Edison, transformed itself into a black box of finance businesses, dragging itself down as a result. The total market value of major airlines like American, United, and Delta is less than the value of their loyalty programs, in which people get miles by flying and by spending with airline-branded credit cards. In 2020, American Airlines' loyalty program was valued at $18–$30 billion while the market capitalization of the entire company was $14 billion.[12] This suggests that the actual airline business—flying people from one place to another—is valuable only insofar as it gets people to participate in a loyalty program.

The main result of financialization is best explained by the "Cantillon effect," which means that money creation, over a long period of time, redistributes wealth upward to the already rich.[13] This effect was first described in the eighteenth century by Richard Cantillon after he observed the results of introducing a paper money system. He noted that the first people to receive the new money saw their incomes rise, while the last to receive it saw a decline in their purchasing power because of consumer price inflation.[14] The first to receive newly created money are banks and other financial institutions. They are called "Cantillon insiders," a term coined by Nick Szabo, and they get the most benefit. But all owners of assets—including stocks, real estate, even a home—are enriched to some extent by the Cantillon effect. Those who own a lot of assets benefit the most and financial assets tend to increase in value faster than other types, but all gain value. This is a version of the Matthew Principle, taken from Jesus' Parable of the Sower: to those who have, more will be given. The more assets you own, the faster your wealth will increase.

Meanwhile, the people without assets fall behind, as asset prices rise faster than incomes. Inflation hawks have long worried that America's decades-long policy of running large government deficits combined with easy money from the Fed will lead to runaway inflation that beggars average Americans. This was seen clearly in 2022 after the massive increase in dollars created by the Fed in 2020 and 2021. Even so, they've mostly been looking for inflation in the wrong place. It's true that the prices of many raw materials, such as lumber and corn, have soared recently, followed by much more broad-based inflation in everything from food to rent, but inflation in the form of asset price bubbles has been with us for much longer. Those bubbles pop and prices drop, but the next bubble raises them even higher. Asset price inflation benefits asset owners, but not the people with few or no assets, like young people just starting out and finding themselves unable to afford to buy a home.

The Cantillon effect has been one of the main vectors of increased wealth concentration over the last forty years. One way that the large banks use their insider status is by getting short-term loans from the Federal Reserve and lending the money back to the government by buying longer-term treasuries at a slightly higher interest rate and locking in a profit. Their position in the economy essentially guarantees them profits, and their size and political influence protect them from losses. We've seen the pattern of private profits and public losses clearly in the savings and loan crisis of the 1980s, and in the financial crisis of 2008. Banks and speculators made a lot of money in the years leading up to the crisis, and when the losses on their bad loans came due, they got bailouts.

The Cantillon economy creates moral hazard in that large companies, especially financial institutions, can privatize profits and socialize losses. Insiders, and shareholders more broadly, can reap massive gains when the bets they make with the company's capital pay off. When the bets go bad, the company gets bailed out. Alan Krueger, the chief economist at the Treasury Department in the Obama administration, explained years later why banks and not homeowners were rescued from the fallout of the mortgage crisis: "It would have been extremely unfair, and created problems down the road to bail out homeowners who were irresponsible and took on homes they couldn't afford."[15] Krueger glossed over the fact that the banks had used predatory and deceptive practices to initiate risky loans, and when they lost hundreds of billions of dollars—or trillions by some estimates—they were bailed out while homeowners were kicked out. That callous indifference alienates and radical-izes the forgotten men and women who have been losing ground.

Most people know about the big bailouts in 2008, but the system that joins private profit with socialized losses regularly creates incentives for slop-piness and corruption. The greed sometimes takes ridiculous forms. But once that culture takes over, it poisons everything it touches. Starting in 2002, for example, Wells Fargo began a scam in which it paid employees to open more than 3.5 million unauthorized checking accounts, savings accounts, and credit cards for retail customers.[16] By exaggerating growth in the number of active retail accounts, the bank could give investors a false picture of the health of its retail business. It also charged those customers monthly service fees, which contributed to the bottom line and bolstered the numbers in quarterly earn-ings reports to Wall Street. Bigger profits led to higher stock prices, enriching senior executives whose compensation packages included large options grants. John Stumpf, the company's CEO from 2007 to 2016, was forced to resign and disgorge around $40 million in repayments to Wells Fargo and fines to the federal government. Bloomberg estimates that he retained more than $100 million. Wells Fargo paid a $3 billion fine, which amounted to less than two months' profit, as the bank's annual profits averaged around $19.7 billion from 2017 to 2019. And this was for a scam that lasted nearly fifteen years.

What is perhaps most absurd and despicable about this scheme is that Wells Fargo was conducting it during and even after the credit bubble, when the bank received billions of dollars in bailouts from the govern-ment. The alliance between the largest corporations and the state leads to corrupt and abusive practices. This is one of the second-order effects of the Cantillon economy.

Another effect is that managers respond to short-term financial incentives in a way that undermines the long-term vitality of their own company. An ex-cessive focus on quarterly earnings is sometimes referred to as short-termism. Senior managers, especially at the C-suite level of public companies, are largely compensated with stock options, so they have a strong incentive to see the stock rise. In principle, a rising stock price should reflect a healthy, growing, profitable company. But managers figured out how to game the system: with the Fed keeping long-term rates low, corporations can borrow money at a much lower rate than the expected return in the stock market. Many companies have taken on long-term debt to finance stock repurchases, which helps inflate the stock price. This practice is one reason that corporate debt has soared since 1980.

The Cantillon effect distorts resource allocation, incentivizing rent seeking in the financial industry and rewarding nonfinancial companies for becoming stealth financial firms. Profits are quicker and easier in finance than in other industries. As a result, many smart, ambitious people go to Wall Street instead of trying to invent useful products or seeking a new source of abundant power—endeavors that don't have as much assurance of a payoff. How different might America be if the incentives were structured to reward the people who put their brainpower and energy into those sorts of projects rather than into quantitative trading algorithms and financial derivatives of home mortgages.

While the financial industry does well, the manufacturing sector lags. Because of Covid-19, Americans discovered that the United States has very limited capacity to make the personal protective equipment that was in such urgent demand in 2020. We do not manufacture any of the most widely prescribed antibiotics, or drugs for heart disease or diabetes, nor any of the chemical precursors required to make them. A close look at other vital industries reveals the same penury. The rare earth minerals necessary for batteries and electronic screens mostly come from China because we have intentionally shuttered domestic sources or failed to develop them. We're dependent on Taiwan for the computer chips that go into everything from phones to cars to appliances, and broken supply chains in 2021 led to widespread shortages. The list of necessities we import because we have exported our manufacturing base goes on.

Financialization of the economy amplifies the resource curse that has come with dollar supremacy. Richard Cantillon described a similar effect when he observed what happened to Spain and Portugal when they acquired large amounts of silver and gold from the New World. The new wealth raised prices, but it went largely into purchasing imported goods, which ruined the manufactures of the state and led to a general impoverishment. In America today, a fiat currency that serves as the world's reserve is the resource curse that erodes the manufacturing base while the financial sector flourishes. Since the dollar's value was formally dissociated from gold in 1976, it now rests on American economic prosperity, political stability, and military supremacy. If these advantages diminish relative to competitors, so will the value of the dollar.

Dollar supremacy has also encouraged a debt-based economy. Federal debt as a share of GDP has risen from around 38 percent in 1970 to nearly 140 percent in 2020. Corporate debt has had peaks and troughs over those decades, but each new peak is higher than the last. In the 1970s, total nonfinancial corporate debt in the United States ranged between 30 and 35 percent of GDP. It peaked at about 43 percent in 1990, then at 45 percent with the dot-com bubble in 2001, then at slightly higher with the housing bubble in 2008, and now it's approximately 47 percent. As asset prices have climbed faster than wages, consumer debt has soared from 43.2 percent of GDP in 1970 to over 75 percent in 2020.[17] Student loan debt has soared even faster in recent years: in 2003 it totaled $240 billion—basically a rounding error—but by 2020 the sum had ballooned to six times as large, at $1.68 trillion, which amounts to around 8 percent of GDP. Increases in aggregate debt throughout society are a predictable result of the Cantillon effect in a financialized economy.

The Cantillon effect generates big gains for those closest to the money spigot, and especially those at the top of the financial industry, while the people furthest away fall behind. Average families find it more difficult to buy a home and maintain a middle-class life. In 90 percent of U.S. counties today, the median-priced single-family home is unaffordable on the median wage. One of the ways that families try to make ends meet is with the promiscuous use of credit. It's one of the reasons that personal and household debt levels have risen across the board. People borrow money to cover the gap between expectations and reality, hoping that economic growth will soon pull them out of debt. But for many, it's a trap they can never escape.

FIGURE FOUR

Ratio of Nonfinancial Corporate Debt Outstanding to GDP

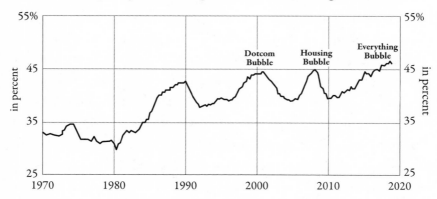

Source: FRED Economic Data, St. Louis Fed, https://fred.stlouisfed.org/graph/?g=VLW.

FIGURE FIVE

Historical National Student Loan Debt Balance

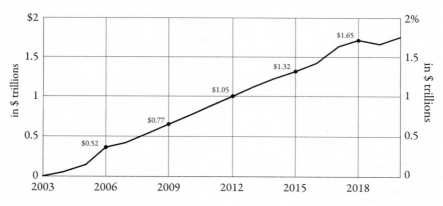

Source: Melanie Hanson, "Average Student Loan Debt by Year," EducationData.org.

Another way that families have tried to keep up is by adding a second income. In 2018, over 60 percent of families were two-income households, up from about 30 percent in 1970. This change is not a result of simple desire to do wage-work outside the home, or of "increased opportunities," as we are often told. The reason is that it now takes two incomes to support the needs of a middle-class family, whereas fifty years ago it required only one. As more people entered the labor market, the value of labor declined, setting up a vicious cycle in which a second income came to be more necessary. China's entry into the World Trade Organization in 2001 put more downward pressure on the value of labor.

When people laud the fact that we have so many more two-income families—generally meaning more women working outside the home—as evidence that there are so many great opportunities, what they're really doing is retconning something usually done out of economic necessity. Needing twice as much labor to get the same result is the opposite of what happens when productivity growth is robust. It also means that the raising of children is increasingly outsourced. That's not improvement.

Another response to stagnant wages is to delay family formation and have fewer children. In 1960, the median age of first marriage was about 20.5 years. In 2010 it was approximately 27, and in 2020 it was an all-time high of over 29.[18] At the same time, the total fertility rate of American women was dropping: from 3.65 in 1960 down to 2.1, a little below replacement level, in the early 1970s. Currently it hovers around 1.8. Some people may look on this approvingly, being worried about overpopulation and the impact of humans on the environment. But when people choose to have few or no children, it is usually not a political choice. That doesn't mean it is simply a "revealed preference," a lower desire for a family and children, rather than a reflection of personal challenges or how people view their prospects for the future. Surely it's no coincidence that the shrinking of families has happened at the same time that real wages have stagnated or grown very slowly, while the costs of housing, health care, and higher education have soared.

The fact that American living standards have broadly stagnated, and for some segments of the population have declined, should be cause for real concern to the ruling class. Americans expect economic mobility and a chance for prosperity. Without it, many will believe that the government has failed to deliver on its promises. The Chinese Communist Party is regarded as legitimate by the Chinese people because it has presided over a large, broad, multigenerational rise in living standards. If stagnation or decline in the United States is not addressed effectively, it will threaten the legitimacy of the governing institutions. But instead of meeting the challenge head-on, America's political and business leaders have pursued policies and strategies that exacerbate the problem. Woke policies in academia, government, and big business have created a stultifying environment that is openly hostile to heterodox views. Witness the response to views on Covid that contradicted official opinion. And all this happens against a backdrop of destructive fiscal and monetary policies.

Low growth and low mobility tend to increase political instability when the legitimacy of the political order is predicated upon opportunity and egalitarianism. One source of national unity has been the understanding that every individual has an equal right to pursue happiness, that a dignified life is well within reach of the average person, and that the possibility of rising higher is open to all. When too many people feel they cannot rise, and when even the basics of a middle-class life are difficult to secure, disappointment can breed a sense of injustice that leads to social and political conflict. At first, that conflict acts as a drag on what American society can accomplish. Left unchecked, it will consume energy and resources that could otherwise be put into more productive activities. Thwarted personal aspirations are often channeled into politics and zero-sum factional conflict. The rise of identity politics represents a redirection of the frustrations born of broken dreams. But identity politics further divides us into hostile camps.

We've already seen increased social unrest lately, and more is likely to follow. High levels of social and political conflict are dangerous for a country that hopes to maintain a popular form of government. Not so long ago, we could find unity in civic rituals and were encouraged to be proud of our country. Now our history is denigrated in schools and by other sensemaking institutions, leading to cultural dysphoria, social atomization, and alienation. In exchange you can choose your pronouns, which doesn't seem like such a great trade. Just as important as regaining broad-based material prosperity and rising standards of living—perhaps more important—is unifying the nation around a common understanding of who we Americans are and why we're here.

2

SENSEMAKING, HYPERREALITY, AND FRAYED CONSENSUS

EVERY CIVILIZATION IS SHAPED BY BROADLY SHARED ANSWERS to questions concerning truth and values: How do we make sense of the world? Which authorities do we trust? What framing of life is normative? Whom do we honor as heroes? The answers to such questions are becoming more and more contested in America today, and one reason is that the modern media world cultivates division while it overwhelms our sensemaking abilities. The accelerating flow of media content floods our senses with information and images that generate a confusing simulacrum of reality. In the "information age," we might think we know more than our forebears, but often we are disoriented as well as angry and divided.

For most of history, people experienced the world directly and made sense of it through the family, religion, and the clan, tribe, kingdom, or nation. Those sources of authority remain dispositive for some people today, but we have many other competing sources of information and knowledge. Our experience of the world has become increasingly mediated by people we don't know, through a variety of advancing communication technologies: the printing press, radio, television, the internet, and other digital technologies.

We experience much of life through a screen that bombards us with countless ideas, symbols, and images, which together form a representation of reality.

We are inundated with news reports, images, ideas, and symbols all day, every day. The average person sees 4,000–10,000 ads per day in 7.5 hours spent consuming media.[1] We are exposed daily to hundreds of news stories, spanning a huge range of subjects: sports, weather, celebrity gossip, what the president said today, whether eggs are good or bad for you this year, and so on. It's a modern conceit that all this information creates wisdom. We may be expected to hold opinions on any number of assorted topics: What did LeBron James say today? Did you see what Turkey did in Libya? How about the plight of the Uighurs? Are the schools any good in Afghanistan? How dangerous is the latest variant of Covid?

The flood of stories and images blasted at us around the clock can overpower our sensemaking abilities while creating an illusion of knowledge and wisdom. Symbols and images become untethered from the objective reality behind them and create their own reality. Consider the experience of having witnessed something firsthand and then seeing a news report about the event. It is never the same thing. Now multiply this disparity across all kinds of news stories, from the most mundane to the most important. How reliable is the representation of the world that we are getting? Even objective metrics we often rely upon, like GDP and productivity figures, can become untethered from reality if we misread what they actually tell us.

As our society has become more complex and our experience of the world more mediated by technology, a simulacrum of reality competes with objective reality and creates what has been called *hyperreality*. Jean Baudrillard, one of the first people to develop the idea, gave the analogy of cartographers creating a map of a great empire on a 1:1 scale, so eventually it covers the whole empire. The simulacrum effectively replaces the reality. In a state of hyperreality, consciousness is unable to distinguish a simulation from the reality behind it.

Today's information and entertainment media and communication technologies offer "experiences more intense and involving than the scenes of banal everyday life." Televised sports, media simulations, amusement parks, virtual reality games, social networking sites, and so on create a world that seems "more real than real." The media-saturated consciousness becomes "narcoticized" and "mesmerized" by spectacle, until "the concept of meaning itself (which depends on stable boundaries, fixed structures, shared consensus) dissolves." Baudrillard compared a person living in the state of hyperreality to "the schizophrenic [who] is open to everything and lives in the most extreme confusion." He wrote that in 1988, before the advent of 24/7 cable news, the internet, social media, and ubiquitous screens.

Both the complexity of our societies and the pace at which information flows have increased dramatically in a short period of time. It is the latter that has proved to be the more powerful solvent, overwhelming our ability to make sense of it all. The technology-enabled "ecstasy of communication," to use Baudrillard's term, paradoxically has distorting and disorienting effects that can hamper judgment and decision making. The media-generated hyperreality also has alienating effects that make it harder to establish and maintain normal social relationships. Many people today have hundreds or thousands of friends and followers associated with their social media accounts, but few friends in real life. It is not uncommon for people to construct the illusion of personal relationships with the celebrities, politicians, athletes, and influencers they follow online.

There are other antisocial effects of media hyperreality too. Television news can easily draw us into a hyperbolic narrative and make us agitated, but social media does it even more powerfully, and largely on purpose. Every platform is designed to create an addictive experience that absorbs as much of a user's time as possible, with the most sophisticated tools of psychological manipulation known to man. They track when you are on the platform, where you are, what you look at and for how long, your likes and shares and comments, and much more. This information is used to determine what ads you are shown and what content will keep you on the platform longer, so you will see more ads. What keeps your attention is what engages your passions and especially what makes you outraged. Content creators know this too. The sensemaking role once filled by religion has largely been taken over by media. But whereas traditional religion sought unity, today's media experience is geared to trigger conflict, through technology to hack the human brain.

The political polarization and accompanying culture war that are so much discussed—and are essentially two aspects of the same phenomenon—have multiple causes, including economic, class, racial, ethnic, ideological, and spiritual divisions. But one overlooked source of discord is that we are overwhelmed with information, and much of the media we consume is deliberately divisive. On top if this is the disorienting effects of hyperreality, like a fog of war that results from sensory overload and can make people more aggressive, slower to process information, and less able distinguish fact from hype. We are seeing more intensely emotional discord, along with deepening divisions on questions of fundamental principles and authoritative sources of knowledge.

Since the earliest human communities, religion has been a fundamental unifying force and a way of making sense of the world. It provides a common understanding of life's purposes and mysteries, and a moral code. When people share a sense of the transcendent and of what they are called to honor, the result is more social cohesion and a capacity for collective action. It produces *asabiyya*. Many of the most noteworthy achievements of past civilizations were done in the name of religion: the Sumerian ziggurats, the Egyptian pyramids, ancient henges and mounds around the world, the Christian cathedrals all over Europe, the Great Buddha of Kamakura and the Giant Buddha of Leshan, Angkor Wat in Cambodia, the Aztec temples of Mexico. On the edge of the Bosporus, Hagia Sophia testifies to the permanence of religion even through its changes over the centuries: it was built as a Christian church in 537, became a mosque when Constantinople fell to the Ottomans in 1453, was turned into a museum in 1935 when Turkey became officially secular, and then became a mosque again in 2020.

The long spans of time over which some great religious buildings have been constructed is another testament to the endurance of religious commitment. The Duomo of Milan, started in 1386, was almost continuously under construction until its completion in 1965. The building of this immense cathedral was a communal project for a very long time. Perhaps it's natural that the people of Milan took the long view, as the Po Valley in which their city sits is one of Europe's longest-inhabited and most consistently prosperous regions. The Duomo, the third largest church in the world, attracts millions of visitors every year and remains a source of civic pride. The main façade underwent renovation recently, and the ongoing cost of maintenance has required voluntary contributions from the public as well as governmental support. But the benefit that the cathedral offers cannot be captured in economic terms: beautiful structures and spaces make life more pleasant and draw people to them. Pride in the Duomo adds to the social fabric that unifies the people who live around it. We do not have a good way of measuring beauty or civic pride, but we know they are important.

Milan's cathedral is an expression of religious solidarity, which has been a feature of every civilization that has sustained itself and prospered over a long period of time, and especially those that have been at the forefront of world affairs. For example, the ancient Roman authorities accepted many gods, but the pantheon was the state religion and its rites were often closely associated with the state. It's revealing that while Roman religion incorporated the gods of conquered nations, it rejected Yahweh—the God of the Bible—who made claims to exclusivity. The Roman authorities' relations with Jews and Christians were uneasy, alternating between toleration and persecution, until Christianity supplanted the old gods and was made the official state religion.

The western half of a divided Roman Empire soon collapsed, but the eastern part endured until 1453. The Byzantine Empire was multiethnic and generally tolerant of minority religions, though Eastern Orthodox Christianity was the religion of the state, in what Sir Dimitri Obolensky called "a multinational community of faith."[2] The emperor appointed the

Patriarch of Constantinople as the leading official of the church, but the emperor himself was ultimately head of both church and state.

China is not typically seen as an example of religious unity, but Confucianism, Taoism, and Buddhism—the "three teachings"—have coexisted and often complemented each other for many centuries, while other religions have largely been suppressed. Hinduism has been dominant in most of India for millennia. Today, around 80 percent of Indians are Hindu.

The United States has a foundational patrimony of Christian civilization, though that legacy has lately been fading away. Some people lament its passing, others welcome it, but no one denies it. Yet there is still an essentially Protestant substrate to American culture. One way to understand American gentry liberalism and its crusading, moralizing zeal is as the secular descendant of New England Puritanism. Opposed to this secular gospel are the many millions of faithful Christians in America. Non-Christian religions have a bigger place in America than ever before, but it's really the rise of the "nones," people with no religion, that defines the age.

Religious pluralism—the lack of either a state religion or a culturally superdominant religion—is often cited as one of the benefits of liberalism. Freedom of conscience is understood by many people as a moral imperative, but one that also has practical benefits: a general spirit of tolerance for other beliefs is supposed to reduce violence and promote social stability, as everyone benefits from mutual tolerance. There's a market logic to this civic transaction: I leave you alone, you leave me alone, and we both benefit. That's good as long as the understanding lasts—which is only until one group senses it can win if it moves first, or believes there is a moral imperative to overturn the compact.

If this compact is going to hold in America, there are some realities we need to face head-on. The first is that there are no historical examples of a large, imperial nation without a unifying religion, whether a national cult, an established church, or simply a religion practiced by a supermajority of the population and enjoying official deference. In fact, there are really no examples of such a thing ever being attempted. It's a thoroughly modern concept created by Enlightenment philosophers who wanted to subordinate revealed religion to the power of pure reason.

Another reality is that participatory government has been relatively rare in human history, and the early examples were small-scale, such as the Greek city-states and later the Italian urban republics. Every society requires groups with different priorities to subordinate their desires and interests to the needs of the whole—city, state, or nation. In a participatory government, citizens expect a voice in public policy, but are to respect the interests of others and defer to collective decisions. As the size of a state increases and more divergent beliefs and interests are incorporated, there are more points of friction. The society grows more susceptible to internal conflict and triggering events that could result in systemic breakdown.

The United States is far more complex today than it was at its founding, with many more differing beliefs and cultural values to be encompassed in peaceful coexistence. The main challenge before America is how to prevent our differences from tearing us apart. Representative Ro Khanna (D-CA), who represents Silicon Valley and was the cochairman of Bernie Sanders's campaign for president in 2020, recognizes how unusual our situation is historically:

> The challenge of building a multiracial, multiethnic democracy is unprecedented in world history. For all the talk from Trudeau in Canada about multiculturalism, or the lectures of inclusion from Australia or Great Britain, remember that those societies are over 80 percent white. They also have never had a person of color as head of state or immigrants running as many of their major corporations. In comparison, the United States is 60 percent white, and we literally have people from every corner of the globe. Our politics are polarized because our political project is hard. How can we find a common political language and political religion, rooted in our founding principles, that binds people of very different faiths, histories, and ancestries. Post 1965 America is the true test of whether a nation can

be conceived on an allegiance to a philosophical idea. The challenge is even steeper as we undertake this effort during a time of economic transformation to a digital age. A nation that can produce Obama, Trump, and AOC within a few cycles of each other is one that is figuring out how every American will find a dignified place in our national story. We have not arrived yet to our destination, but we will. And when we do in my lifetime hopefully, this feat will be America's greatest and noblest contribution to human civilization.[3]

Is there a "common political language and political religion" that can give every American "a dignified place in our national story"? Khanna's optimism is heartening, but the challenge of finding a unifying political language is immense.

G. K. Chesterton, trying to explain the nature of America in 1922, called it "a nation with the soul of a church." The United States was "the only nation in the world that is founded on a creed," one that was articulated "with dogmatic and even theological lucidity in the Declaration of Independence." When outsiders like himself observed the existence of this unique concept, wrote Chesterton, "We say that the Americans are doing something heroic or doing something insane, or doing it in an unworkable or unworthy fashion, instead of simply wondering what the devil they are doing." The American civic creed that had grown up in the eighteenth and nineteenth centuries as a competitor with the Christian roots put down by seventeenth-century settlers—reflected in documents like Dale's Code and the Mayflower Compact—became a replacement or a stand-in for an established church.

The civic creed undergirds America's idea of itself as a rights-based society where government exists at first to protect preexisting rights, but inevitably expands its horizon to include newly discovered rights. American political discourse is filled with the language of rights, in which liberty and equality are to be balanced in the service of natural justice. The political

Left places more emphasis on equality and the Right on liberty, but they agree that these are the essential principles to be maximized in a just society. If it's left there, that amounts to mere abstraction; either a statement of high-minded principles or just breezy platitudes. But Americans are a practical people and there is a pervasive belief that the application of these ideas will improve people's lives. Or they should, if they are to mean anything. Applied egalitarianism is supposed to provide broad-based opportunity, so that living a dignified, productive life is the norm and does not require extraordinary talent, effort, or luck.

This is the civil religion that is supposed to unify the nation and act as a lubricant between competing factions or groups. It was intended to reduce social friction so it doesn't spark violence that brings the whole contraption crashing down. A civil religion might be able to do that under the right circumstances, but can't do it alone.

The term "civil religion" itself points to the problem; it is a neologism that suggests the merger of religion and politics to create a secular creed. Some people think this creed supplements true religion in the public sphere, but in reality it is a competitor that cannot tolerate any other gods. The attempt to replace true religion with civil religion can be seen clearly when Nancy Pelosi talked about the protests that took place on January 6, 2020 as a "desecration" of "the sacred temple of democracy." Can so-called civil religion fill the same social, cultural, and political role as revealed religion? History provides no examples. Do people even really want this type of totalizing "civil religion" or is it more natural simply to have politics and true religion?

The political problem is that when the stakes of a conflict are high enough and the disagreements are over fundamental ideas of right and wrong, civil religion alone simply can't carry the weight. It's ultimately insufficient to keep the peace when there are fundamental moral disagreement about how we should live. That's why civil religion has needed silent partners to make it work as a unifying force. In America it has had a few: a foundational patrimony of Christian civilization and a predominantly

Christian understanding of public and private ethics, and a long period of essentially nonstop economic growth. These two things have contributed much to domestic tranquility and national harmony, but most of the credit has gone to civil religion, which is primarily an ideological construct. Material prosperity has been an additional lubricant that has kept the system working.

When prosperity is increasing and broadly shared, it's easier to work through differences and find compromises because everyone has too much to lose from conflict. But stagnation, which leads to concentrations of power and wealth, heightens the contradictions within the system itself. America has been fortunate that its entire history has coincided with the greatest sustained increase in living standards in human history, powered by sustained advances in science and technology. It is no coincidence that as those advances have slowed since the 1960s and been combined with declining religiosity and all the challenges that accompany a rapidly diversifying society, the result is more social friction and increasing political and cultural polarization.

Material scarcity has often been a cause of conflict within societies and has precipitated violence, social conflict, decay, and war. Is scarcity a problem for the United States today? Food is now so plentiful that obesity is far more common than starvation. Energy from legacy sources is abundant for now, but demand is increasing rapidly and pricing is volatile. Water shortages in western states have sometimes stirred up conflict. Other resources that are key to our way of life and our prosperity are scarce, such as the rare earth minerals needed for batteries and electronic screens. There can be shortages in manufactured goods too, such as the computer chips that make our devices run, or the pharmaceutical drugs that many people rely upon. Even basic food products sometimes ran short during the supply-chain crisis that began in 2021.

Technology is a way to increase what we get from available resources and to raise living standards. When productivity growth slows or stalls, more people will feel scarcity. In the absence of some other unifying force, scarcity in the necessities of life—even if they are first-world needs like iPhone chips—can lead to social conflict, and eventually to political dysfunction.

America has uniquely relied on growth and material abundance as a basis for our national identity and social cohesion, and as a measure of civilizational success. Most great civilizations through history did not enjoy the level of technology-fueled growth that occurred in the last few centuries, yet they flourished. Their people prospered and lived happy, fulfilling lives. Effective political leadership can make the best of prevailing circumstances and available resources, including the people's resourcefulness. A vital political system is one that secures the lives and improves or at least maintains the living standards of the people. It promotes national solidarity, the capacity for collective action, strong families, and a sense of purpose and satisfaction.

Republican governance in late medieval Florence, along with a growing commercial economy, nurtured a vibrant culture marked by civic pride and an explosion of creativity. A society can have limited natural advantages but thrive because of wise political choices and energetic action. For example, the Netherlands, which also had a republican form of government, was built to a considerable extent on land reclaimed from the sea over the centuries through an extensive system of dikes and drainage canals. Hong Kong has been an outstanding modern example of building prosperity on scant natural resources.

On the other hand, a country can have many natural advantages and thrive for a time but then fall into political disorder. For example, Argentina has abundant mineral resources and was considered a developed nation from the time of its independence in 1818 until the early twentieth century. The port of Buenos Aires became an important trading center, and the city has a Parisian feel with its self-consciously French architecture and the parks and plazas designed by Jules Charles (Carlos) Thays. Argentina boasted the tenth highest per capita income in the world in 1913.[4] As late as 1962, its per capita income was higher than that of Japan, Austria, Spain, or Italy.[5] But political dysfunction had already launched a cycle of military coups and juntas and dictatorships alternating with efforts to restore constitutional governance. Argentina has bounced from one political or economic crisis to another for decades, never quite regaining its footing. While it still has one of the strongest economies in Latin America, per capita income is now about half what it is in Japan and Austria, so ambitious Argentines look for opportunities abroad.

The trajectory of Argentina is a cautionary tale of what can happen when a government becomes the focus of widespread discontent and cannot maintain an orderly transfer of power. The United States is a much larger country and remains the single greatest economic and military power. This means that Argentine-style political turmoil would play out on a bigger scale here and likely result in a deeper fall, with wider repercussions.

There are already troubling signs of deteriorating faith in the American political system. Three of the six presidential elections since 2000 have been viewed as illegitimate by a sizable portion of the country. The first was George W. Bush's election on the back of a Supreme Court decision giving him Florida's electoral votes in an extremely tight race. Next, as many as 80 percent of Democrats believed that the Trump campaign colluded with Russia to win the 2016 election.[6] In recent polls, 73 percent of Republicans said that the 2020 election was not decided fairly. This level of distrust in the electoral system is a flashing red light.

Americans are socially sorting themselves in a more partisan way than in the past. In a bygone era, Americans commonly did not want their children to marry someone of a different religion; now a growing number look askance at political intermarriage. A poll by Gallup in 1958 found that 72 percent of Americans didn't care about the political party of their child's prospective spouse; a survey in 2017 found that only 45 percent were not concerned that their children might marry someone outside their political faith.[7] This indicates the rising tide of what is sometimes called "hyperpartisanship," which can be a source of systemic breakdown if not arrested. It points to the weakness of civil religion as a foundation for national vitality. National identity is stronger than civil religion, especially when there is fundamental disagreement over the tenets of the faith.

The growth of hyperpartisanship coincides with a broader decline in social trust—trust in government, in authoritative institutions, and in other Americans. A study of different aspects of social trust by the Pew Research Center showed that in general it has declined with each successive generation, but there are also striking differences along lines of education and income. Among people without a college education, 43 percent are "low-trusters" and only 15 percent are "high-trusters." Among people with postgraduate degrees, 20 percent fall into the low-trust group while 33 percent are high-trusters. The comparison by income yields similar numbers: in the group earning $30,000 or less, 45 percent are low-trusters and only 13 percent high-trusters; among those earning $75,000 or more, the numbers are 25 percent and 30 respectively. If your life is going fairly well, you are more likely to have faith in the system and in people around you. Why not? It's working for you. Though Pew did not include it in their study, one suspects that the high-trust group might be even a bit larger at incomes over $200,000. Economic insecurity appears to corrode social trust, and if each generation is falling behind the previous one, we are entering a danger zone of collapsing trust in the American system.

"A two-party democracy cannot provide stable and effective government unless there is a large measure of ideological consensus among its citizens," wrote Anthony Downs in his study of democracy in 1957.[8] That's true as far as it goes, but it leaves unanswered the question of how such a consensus is achieved. What does it rest on? What are the likely points of friction, and how can they be smoothed over? Material stress can undermine consensus, but existential threats can foster a unified response. Conversely, a strong consensus on fundamental principles helps a society navigate through difficult times.

This is where the broad concept of *asabiyya* is more useful than Downs's idealistic approach to democratic politics, because it better encompasses all the different aspects of human life. Viewing politics as purely or mostly ideological is one of the conceits of liberalism. The fundamental questions of national politics are not just ideological; they are also questions of who we are, how we shall live, and what we shall do together. There are religious, familial, and cultural answers to those questions that existed before and are independent of ideology. These are sometimes called folkways, and they are a source of enduring strength for a society. The ideological and transactional natures of the liberal order actively corrode folkways, religion, and family, but these things are natural to human life. They cannot be extinguished. We can draw strength from them to meet the challenges ahead, as did Americans of earlier generations.

But decay need not lead to defeat. In the years immediately after independence, America was amazingly dynamic, but also shambolic. The country was in a deep economic recession. Great Britain was closed to American exports, as were the British sugar colonies in the Caribbean. The dollar was essentially worthless, primarily because of the massive war debt. From 1785 to 1834, America was on a rollercoaster ride of eleven financial panics, recessions, and depressions that lasted between six months (the 1812 recession) and six years (the depression of 1815–1821). Political divisions were sharp, but the country was growing. Thirteen new states entered the Union, the Louisiana Purchase extended the territory of the United States as far west as Colorado and Montana, and victory in the War of 1812 secured the independence won a generation earlier. Real wages tripled. Median height and life expectancy both increased, as did fertility rates. The country was brimming with optimism and vitality, and Americans were united around a hyperproject of taming a continent and building a nation.[9] For America to regain its vitality, it must undertake large projects that both require and reward bold, successful action. Conquering the frontier required a combination of public and private initiatives both large and small. Later in the book, I will identify some projects that might help us regain our national vitality.

3

INSTITUTIONAL BETRAYAL AND ELITE SOCIOPATHOLOGY

EVERY SOCIETY HAS ELITES, OR AT LEAST A RULING CLASS. This is true even in America, a nation that identifies in part with egalitarian ideals. But there are different ways of defining "elites." The word can refer to people who were born into privilege. It can mean people who have displayed excellence in a particular field, such as science, athletics, the military, or the arts. Or it can denote those who lead the society's dominant gatekeeping or sensemaking institutions, both public and private. In those positions of authority, they effectively become part of a ruling class. We would like those people to be elite in the sense of "excellent" in both ability and character, though often they are incompetent or self-interested yet feel entitled to rule. That's when the terms "ruling class" and "elites" become terms of disdain and derision.

The idea that elites are a natural part of any society may seem contrary to the egalitarian spirit of the age. But those how decry the very concept of elites may be trying to conceal their own ambition to be among the elite, while signaling acceptance of the egalitarian creed. Or they may, quite understandably, be expressing resentment at abuse by a self-serving ruling class—a ruling class that is more of an oligarchy than an aristocracy in the original sense of the word.

In classical political thought, aristocracy meant rule by the best, the *aristos*, who were expected to act for the public good. Though the term "aristocracy" has come to be associated in large measure with a privileged status by birth, it retains an idea of excellence and even *noblesse oblige*. "Oligarchy," on the other hand, is simply rule by the few. Oligarchs are people who have managed to grab power and are not assumed to be characterized by excellence or to have a sense of responsibility to use their power or influence in the public interest.

The best-known example of oligarchs today is the people who parlayed political access into vast personal fortunes in postcommunist Russia. They are in fact called Russian oligarchs, never Russian aristocrats, and they built self-serving commercial empires in the scramble for assets after the Soviet Union imploded. Meanwhile, ordinary Russians suffered through an economic disaster that owed in part to bad advice from Western economists who urged the devaluation of the ruble. Russia during this time exhibited all the measurable indicators of a society in decay: soaring crime, widespread alcoholism and drug use, skyrocketing abortion rates, high infant mortality, and plummeting fertility. A fact that is underappreciated in the West is that the violence, poverty, and despair were the predicate for Vladimir Putin's ascendancy. He is widely popular in Russia and viewed as a legitimate leader because he reestablished order, something that is necessary before any other social goods are possible.

If a society's leaders are incompetent or fail to serve the needs of the public, it leaves more opportunity for the self-interested to exploit access to power for their own advantage. They can reap benefits from public policy while pushing the costs of their private ventures onto the public. When elites who lead government and the sensemaking, gatekeeping institutions view their interests as divergent from the interests of those they are meant to serve, the results can be felt as *institutional betrayal*. The term is used in psychology to describe a response to wrongs that an institution perpetrates upon individuals who depend on it.[1] The harm from institutional betrayal can be both material and psychological.

One example is the pattern of actions leading up to the 2008 financial crisis and directly following it. Big banks and other Wall Street firms created a poisonous stew of predatory mortgages, which they packaged and sold as investment-grade securities, fully knowing that the underlying loans were garbage. It was an immensely profitable fraud that nearly collapsed the global financial system and ushered in the Great Recession. Many people lost their jobs, their homes, their savings, and their credit. The psychological harm came later, when the people who suffered those losses discovered that the banks had known exactly what they were doing. To make things worse, the corruption was rewarded when banks were bailed out by the government and the bankers responsible for the crisis kept their jobs, many with huge bonuses.

Institutional betrayal on that scale is a sign that the people in charge are effectively sociopathic—unconcerned that their behavior may adversely affect other people. Disregard for the well-being of constituents or the wider public can be found in a variety of institutions—government, large corporations, academia, the media, and others. When dominant institutions, public or private, are led by sociopathic elites, a widespread sense of betrayal sets in.

Competent elites can do good when they see their interests as being in harmony with those of the wider society. When elites are inept or self-interested, the institutions they control are not only vectors of decay, but victims too. The Roman Empire provides instructive and colorful examples of both the good and the bad.

With his victory over Mark Antony at the Battle of Actium in 31 BC, Augustus ended the long period of civil war that followed Caesar's assassination and inaugurated the two-century Pax Romana. He famously said that he found Rome a city of bricks and left it a city of marble, and it was true. Under his rule, a serviceable republican capital became an imperial city of unmatched splendor. He built the Forum of Augustus, the Baths of Agrippa, temples all over Rome, and much more. Across the empire, he had neglected temples renovated and modest ones made more glorious, and he encouraged traditional piety. He had roads and aqueducts repaired and new ones built, improving life for ordinary citizens.

Augustus instituted a transparent tax system that stabilized the state's finances. He abolished tax farming, the system through which Rome outsourced tax collection, is it had fostered abuse and political corruption. He set up a more efficient administrative system: for the first time the Eternal City had permanent, professional police and firefighting forces. Among other agencies he created were the Supervisors of Public Property (*curatores locorum publicorum iudicandorum*), a commission of five senators to oversee maintenance of public buildings and temples; the Supervisors for Roads (*curatores viarum*), a commission that oversaw the maintenance of roads; and a courier service (*cursus publicus*) to transport tax revenue and messages as well as officials. Its relay stations were still being used in the sixth century, and the speed of the messengers was unrivaled in Europe until the nineteenth century.[2]

Augustus mandated the purity of the gold aureus and the silver denarius, inaugurating an era of sound money, which facilitated trade. The denarius was 97–98 percent silver during his reign and remained at that level even under Nero (54–68 AD). But by the time of Marcus Aurelius (161–180 AD), it was down to 50 percent silver. And by the time of the imperial crisis in the third century, the silver content plummeted further, reaching 0.5 percent in the reign of Philip the Arab (244–249) and 0.2 percent under Claudius II (268–270).

That deep debasement of Roman coin occurred during what is called the Crisis of the Third Century, when there were twenty-six Roman emperors over a period of fifty years (235–284). They are called the "barracks emperors" because they were mostly military commanders who seized power with the backing of their legions, promising spoils in return for their loyalty. The barracks emperors were constantly under threat of being assassinated and replaced by others like themselves, and at times there were multiple usurpers leading rebellions in the provinces. For this reason, the wealth that came into Rome from across the empire was used first of all to pay off the soldiers who sustained the emperor's power. This was a marked change from the Augustan era with all its public works. The institutions created or reinvigorated by Augustus had been captured by a self-dealing ruling class who were content to operate them for private advantage, to the detriment of the Roman public and Roman civilization. If there was ever a period marked by institutional betrayal and sociopathic elites, this was it.

A shared national identity and purpose can serve to keep the interests of elites aligned with the public good so a nation can build and prosper. The most common bases for a shared identity and purpose are: a) an existential threat that makes group cohesion essential for survival; b) a common religion; and c) a desire for national glory that focuses the nation's energies on cultural achievement or territorial expansion. France and Japan are examples of the former, with their highly developed cultures. The Normans are an example of the latter, establishing a political presence from England to the Levant.

In American history, the period from Reconstruction until around 1960 was remarkably productive. The nation was reunified after the trauma of the Civil War. Some of our top universities were founded, and new enterprises like U.S. Steel, the Ford Motor Company, and Dow Chemical began to transform the nation and the world. America grew from the status of developing nation to that of the world's dominant industrial power, in part because elites saw their fortunes as being rooted in America.

The early Ford Motor Company provides an illustration. In 1914, Henry Ford increased workers' pay to $5 for an eight-hour day, which was double the average wage for a factory worker at the time. He did this for a couple of reasons: he wanted to attract better workers as a means of increasing output, and he wanted his employees to be able to buy a Model-T. The plan worked. In 1913, with its assembly line and conveyor belt, the Ford company produced 170,211 Model-Ts. With better-paid workers, the number climbed in subsequent years, reaching over two million in 1923. Technology reduced the amount of labor needed to build a car, so workers could be paid at a higher rate and could afford to buy what they were building.

This bargain was the basis of the American middle class: entrepreneurial innovation plus a commitment to paying workers enough to buy the cutting-edge products they were making. It's a simple equation that creates a healthy, self-sustaining ecosystem. Yes, there is a ruling class, and yes, they'll be making more money than laborers and will have more influence in society and politics. But they'll also be rooted and grounded in America by their dependence on the rest of the country. And yes, there were abuses and conflicts, such as the dispute with labor organizers that led to the Battle of the Overpass at Ford's Rouge River Plant in 1937, or the attempt by the International Workers of the World (the Wobblies) to assassinate the oil executive J. Edgar Pew by blowing up his Tulsa home, or the conditions in the Kentucky coal mines that led Florence Reece to write "Whose Side Are You On?" and inspired many other miners' ballads. But on the whole, the system worked well for ordinary Americans.

Henry Ford increased productivity at his company by adding the conveyor belt to the assembly line, which allowed for higher pay, attracting the best workers, who increased productivity further while building a transformative product they could buy. Everybody won. What broke up this arrangement was globalization—enabled by advances in transportation, communication, and finance—which brought competition with cheaper imports. If there isn't new technology that significantly increases productivity, firms will seek to drive down labor prices, and the easiest way to do it was by sending those well-paying jobs abroad in order to take advantage of cheap foreign labor. As productivity growth slowed down, those discrete decisions by individual firms metastasized. Wages stagnated or grew very slowly in real terms for the middle class, while wealth concentrated at the top. Employers were doing well, but American workers became less able to buy the products they were making and found it more difficult to purchase a home and support children.

That knock-on effect of exporting jobs undermines the foundations of society, but it is not reflected in the conventional measures of a nation's economic health, GNP or GDP. Sir James Goldsmith, the French-British financier who made a fortune in the 1970s and 1980s in what would now be called private equity, noticed what was happening in 1994:

> GNP only measures activities in the formal economy which give rise to a monetary transaction. Therefore, economic growth can be increased by simply monetizing the informal economy and absorbing it into the official economy. That means destroying the informal economy because it removes it from the traditional framework in which it is embedded, thereby disrupting and destabilizing family relationship and local communities.[3]

But liberal triumphalism was still ascending and no one listened.

Slow productivity growth and accelerating globalization together have undercut the prospects of the American middle class, and increasingly the prospects of upper-middle-class professionals too. As the interests of the ruling class diverged from those of the rest of the country, the dominant institutions set up incentives that encourage self-serving behavior. This is not to say we should, or can, return to an earlier state of affairs. Nostalgia is debilitating and often idealizes an imperfect past. But there is value in understanding how the vicious cycle of sociopathic incentives began, and piercing through the rationalizations for growing disparities of wealth and power.

Justifications for self-serving behavior by the ruling class have come under various names, such as globalism, neoliberalism, and libertarianism. Often there is both an exoteric and an esoteric story: a myth told in public and an insiders' truth acknowledged only in private.

Eric Weinstein, a mathematician and managing director of Thiel Capital, gave an example of those differing narratives on his podcast. It came from Brad DeLong, an economist who was a Treasury Department official under Lawrence Summers in the Clinton administration and had worked on the North American Free Trade Agreement. The exoteric story was that trade deals like NAFTA benefit everyone because a rising tide lifts all boats. But Weinstein says that DeLong told him an insiders' story, admitting that the people who sold NAFTA to the American public didn't believe what they were saying to sell it. "We knew that it wasn't a simple story of Ricardian equivalence and comparative advantage. We've always known that," DeLong said. When it became clear that NAFTA and similar deals, including China's accession to the World Trade Organization, had beggared the American middle class and wreaked havoc on communities across the country, the exoteric story changed to one of altruistic concern for the poor of other countries. As Weinstein explained it, the argument became: "'Do you know how many peasants in Mexico were helped?' Why do we not talk about the peasants in Mexico now to an American voter and have an academic technocrat say, don't you people understand? You may have been hurt. But my class was helped. And the Mexican peasant was helped. And why are you complaining?" Weinstein described that thinking as "some form of like a mental illness."[4]

Hillary Clinton famously acknowledged the reality of the dual narrative in off-the-record comments leaked to the public. Politics is an "unsavory" process rather like making sausage, she said. "But if everybody's watching, you know, all of the back room discussions and the deals, you know, then people get a little nervous, to say the least. So, you need both a public and a private position."[5] Clinton was pilloried for this remark during the 2016 presidential campaign, but few could have found it shocking that what politicians say in public is not what they say in private.

Some might think they're telling a "noble lie" for a greater good, but elites tell self-serving lies with no resemblance to the noble lie in classical philosophy. When Plato articulated the concept, he was referring to myths that natural leaders tell for the purpose of binding a particular people together. One example is the myth that Cadmus founded the city of Thebes along with warriors who had sprung full-grown from a dragon's teeth. This story gave the Thebans a shared identity, making them not just a group of individuals, but *a people.*

But modern elites don't tell noble lies. They tell petty, self-serving, often transparent lies. They don't increase solidarity or the capacity for collective action, but serve to redirect anger about institutional betrayals and the ways that elites are often insulated from their failures or even rewarded in spite of them. Other lies provoke animosity between people as a strategy for gaining or holding power. Some lies are campaign promises that are likely not intended to be fulfilled.

Every even-numbered year, Republican politicians make promises designed to secure volunteers and votes from the middle class, including many Catholics or evangelical Christians. They might pledge to do something about abortion or religious freedom or the degradation of American culture. Or they might talk about rebuilding America's manufacturing base and raising wages. But after the election, once they've gotten the volunteers, the donations, and the votes they need, those promises go by the wayside. What Republicans have actually done in Washington is support the creation of market-dominant oligopolies in nearly every major industry, and they've done it all in the name of free markets. The top four banks control around 40 percent of all banking assets and enjoy privileged status with the Federal Reserve. Google, Facebook, Amazon, and Microsoft control around 70 percent of all online advertising revenue.[6] Google alone commands around 80 percent of online search revenue.[7] Lately, Republicans have talked a lot about "Big Tech," but with a few exceptions, like Senator Josh Hawley and Governor Ron DeSantis, they appear reluctant to take decisive action. They have a public position and a private position.

Government and large, market-dominant firms both wield immense power. Often their interests align, because of the need for campaign cash, or calculations for a post-political career. There are many opportunities for self-dealing, but the official story is always that the actions are taken in the public interest.

When the hedge fund Long Term Capital Management failed spectacularly in 1997, threatening to take some of the largest banks down with it, the chairman of the Federal Reserve, Alan Greenspan, and the treasury secretary, Robert Rubin (former chairman of Goldman Sachs), stepped in and prevented the collapse of the banks. They took similar measures when speculation in Asian currencies threatened a crisis in 1997, and then after a crisis in Russian debt in 1998, and after the bubble in internet stocks burst in 2000. *Time* magazine, in 1999, dubbed Greenspan and Rubin plus Lawrence Summers, who was the deputy treasury secretary at the time, "the Committee to Save the World." In reality, they were only bailing out speculators, many of whom happened to be their friends and colleagues. And every time the Committee to Save the World and the Federal Reserve monetized speculators' losses, they created moral hazard, so the next bubble grew even larger.

Then we got the housing bubble and the financial crisis of 2008, followed by $152 billion in fiscal stimulus and by revelations that those who had caused so much trouble for millions of people were not penalized. When any one case of incompetence, self-dealing, or corruption is exposed, it might act as little more than a cautionary tale. But when the cases accumulate, and when misbehaving elites are excused or even rewarded, everyone else gains an understanding of how and for whom the system works. The resulting sense of institutional betrayal is destabilizing to the nation.

The housing bubble was swelling around the same time that Enron collapsed in a massive bankruptcy in December 2001 after the Securities and Exchange Commission began looking into its accounting practices. Enron started out as a natural gas company, but in response to deregulatory legislation it transformed into a trader of derivative contracts—which allow producers to mitigate the risks of price fluctuation—for a variety of commodities. Its management began to emphasize aggressive trading to generate cash as quickly as possible. At its peak, Enron had a market capitalization of $60 billion, about seventy times its reported net income, but the company was fraudulently inflating its income as profits began to shrink. The SEC investigation led to multiple criminal charges, and meanwhile the company went into free-fall.

Enron's management had been known in the press as "the smartest guys in the room." *Fortune* magazine named Enron the nation's most innovative company six years running. But there was no innovation at all. They didn't cure cancer or build a hyperdrive. They weren't even trying anything so audacious. If what they said they were doing had been true, it still would have been nothing more than a bunch of people creating and trading pieces of paper that said "you owe me money." Enron was a poster child for the financialization of the economy, reflecting an incentive structure that draws smart people into endeavors that are fundamentally unproductive. But it was also something worse: its business came to be essentially a lie—elaborate and carefully orchestrated, but still just a lie.

The temptation to cut corners and make a quick profit can infect what starts out looking like an effort to create real value. The case of Elizabeth Holmes and Theranos, the company she founded, is a prime example. It appeared to be an inspiring story of a bold, intelligent young woman who set out to invent something beneficial. Holmes studied chemical engineering at Stanford, and participated in genome research, before dropping out in 2003 to launch her business. She claimed to have developed a technology that would enable all kinds of common diagnostic tests to be performed with a single drop of blood drawn by a pinprick, similar to how diabetics monitor their blood glucose.

There was a huge market for such a technology: diagnostic lab testing is a $70-billion-plus business. Holmes raised $700 million from blue-chip venture capital firms. At one point, Theranos had a $10 billion valuation and Holmes a notional net worth of $4.5 billion. She was a celebrity, feted everywhere in her trademark black turtleneck, which was a self-conscious homage to Steve Jobs, a man who actually invented transformational new products. It was a made-for-media story: an attractive young female scientist-entrepreneur with a game-changing innovation in health care.

There were skeptics, but Holmes was savvy about how the game is played. She stacked her board of directors with heavyweights who gave her credibility. At various times they included James Mattis (future secretary of defense), George Shultz (former secretary of state), William Perry (former secretary of defense), Henry Kissinger (former secretary of state), Sam Nunn (former U.S. senator), Bill Frist (former Senate majority leader), Richard Kovacevich (former CEO of Wells Fargo), Riley Bechtel (former CEO of Bechtel Corporation), and David Boies (the lawyer who represented Al Gore in *Bush v. Gore*). There were no medical doctors or scientists aside from Frist, who hadn't practiced medicine in years. The others had no expertise related to the company's business. That gold-plated board was filled with status granters and door openers, offering bipartisan political protection. If Theranos was going anywhere, Medicare would certainly be a big customer.

What's amazing in retrospect is that Holmes raised $700 million from blue-chip venture capital firms when she had no technology to back up her claims. John Ioannidis, a professor at Stanford Medical School, published an article in 2015 noting that there was no peer-reviewed research in medical journals supporting the Theranos technology. The company's own blood-testing device was not accurate. Theranos was using conventional testing machines under the guise of applying its own technology. Various other false claims were made. When HBO aired a television feature on Elizabeth Holmes, it told about the deception behind the rapid rise and ugly collapse of Theranos.

The fraud was the fault of Holmes, of course. But what can we conclude about the professional investors who poured $700 million into her venture? Or the people who gave credibility to Theranos by sitting on its board, with no particular knowledge of the company's business? America's elites are routinely rewarded with plum directorships at major companies, along with stock options. In a sense, they are playing a game, not creating value, nor promoting the creation of value; just scrambling for paydays based on nothing more than their position.

Prominent investors were likewise gulled by Adam Neumann, the founder of WeWork. His audacity put even Elizabeth Holmes and Theranos to shame. Neumann launched WeWork in 2008, describing its business as "flexible workspace solutions." The company rented large amounts of office space from traditional landlords on long-term leases and then subleased it to smaller tenants at a markup. It's potentially a solid, low-margin business, and WeWork was hardly the first of its kind. But Neumann somehow convinced "sophisticated" investors that it was a tech company because tenants could access their accounts through an app, and so it deserved a tech valuation rather than the much lower valuation of a real estate company.

WeWork secured nearly $13 billion in venture capital from marquis investors such as JP Morgan, Goldman Sachs, Benchmark Capital, Harvard, and Softbank Ventures. At one point the company was valued at $47 billion, about half the total value of all publicly traded real estate investment trusts in America. Those are companies that together own hundreds of millions of square feet of premier office buildings, shopping malls, and warehouses, plus most of the top-rated apartment complexes in the country. What's more, there were established companies with the same business model as WeWork, and with profits and strong track records, but valuations a small fraction of how the "sophisticated" investors valued WeWork.

What made WeWork stand out? It was Adam Neumann, who by all accounts was a Svengali. The *Guardian* described him as "the tall, long-haired, barefoot, meat-banning, weed-smoking, tequila-drinking, Kabbalah-studying, experimental school-opening Paltrow-cousin-in-law."[8] In the 1970s he might have had a cult full of young women in a mansion in the Hollywood Hills. His wife, Rebekah, reportedly fired employees if she thought they had "bad vibes." Company meetings took on religious overtones. "There are 150 million orphans in the world," Neumann said at one meeting. "We want to solve this problem and give them a new family: the WeWork family." He said it was the company's mission "to elevate the world's consciousness."[9]

Savvy investors ate it up, while financial media fawned over Neumann and his company. *Time* named WeWork one of the 50 Most Genius Companies of 2018. Around the same time, the *Economist* acknowledged that "sceptics abound," but opined that "there may be more to the startup than meets the eye."[10]

Or maybe less. WeWork lost $2 billion that year. The company filed for a public offering in August 2019, after the *Wall Street Journal* had reported in July that Neumann liquidated $700 million in stock in advance of the IPO, which was not exactly a vote of confidence. Things unraveled quickly amid a realization that WeWork was nothing more than a plain old real estate company, and the music stopped. Neumann was accused of absurd, abusive, and often just weird behavior: serial self-dealing, hiring rappers for no apparent reason with company money, flying around the world on a Gulfstream G650 that the company purchased for him, possibly transporting large amounts of marijuana across international borders, and more.[11] Yet even as the scales were falling from many people's eyes, CNBC wasn't too troubled by the unfolding scandal, instead focusing on the lack of women directors at the foundering company.[12] Regardless of the merits or demerits of the composition of WeWork's board, it is not the most pressing issue when a flim-flam company is torching billions of investor dollars.

Nonetheless, in October 2019, Neumann negotiated a $1.7 billion severance package,[13] including a consulting contract worth $46 million per year. The next month, WeWork laid off 2,400 employees. Another 250 layoffs followed in March. Investors wrote off around 90 percent of the $13 billion invested in the company.

Businesses turn south for many reasons, and experienced investors can make mistakes. Yet it's striking that the brightest lights in the financial firmament have bought into scams like WeWork hook, line, and sinker. While Charles Ponzi's victims were mostly small, inexperienced investors, the people and institutions that poured support enthusiastically into WeWork and Theranos not only possessed credentials and prestige, but *bestowed* them.

A relatively small-dollar enterprise can also become a dramatic example of malinvestment and hype exceeding reality, as shown in the implosion of the Fyre Festival before takeoff. A big music event was planned for the spring of 2017 as a way of promoting a new app called Fyre, which was supposed to allow people to book musicians and other performers directly, bypassing industry agents. The app sounded like a good idea, and Comcast was prepared to invest $25 million in the business.

The Fyre Festival was catnip for Millennials. It was going to take place over two weekends on a Caribbean island, and was promoted by supermodels like Bella Hadid and Emily Ratajkowski, social media influencers like Kendall Jenner, and pop stars like the rapper Ja Rule, who was a partner in the enterprise. For prices ranging from a few thousand dollars up to $400,000 for a luxury package, attendees could mingle with the beautiful people who were promoting the festival, bask under the Caribbean sun, eat gourmet food, hear big-name music acts, and generally luxuriate in a fantasy world of seaside luxury, if only for a few days.

The reality turned out very different. Attendees arrived on the island to find that their luxury accommodations were actually surplus FEMA disaster-recovery tents and that portable bathrooms were scarce. The stages had not been completed. Bands, smelling a rat, were canceling even as ticketholders arrived on the island. In the end, the festival never happened. Excited ticketholders were turned into temporary refugees, stranded on the island and then eventually transported back to the mainland. The promoter was convicted of fraud, sentenced to six years in prison, and ordered to repay $26 million to investors, with other litigation pending.

Fyre brought together many threads of modern American life: the mimetic envy that drives social media, enriches influencers, and empowers companies like Facebook and Snap; the broken venture capital model that currently has too much money and too few serious, game-changing investment opportunities; and Millennials seeking out self-referential "experiences" like traveling to an island festival because they can't afford to buy a house and raise a family. The short-term, transactional mindset of everyone involved is noteworthy. The organizers had to get the models to pose and the photographers to take pictures on the beach, so that bands could be booked, so that Millennials would show up, so that investors would pour in money to launch an app—which they could have launched without any of it.

The pictures were alluring. The Instagram feed looked terrific. Everyone was young, beautiful, and smiling in the sun. The promise was fantastic. The hyperreality was stunning. But when it left the world of bits and returned to the world of atoms, to the real world where people need shelter and food, and musicians need stages to perform on, it all evaporated. Or rather, was never there in the first place. In some sense, everyone involved in promoting Fyre knew it was a lie, but played along anyway on the assumption that at least they would get paid, and surely someone would make it all work. It's part of a broader phenomenon of learned helplessness manifesting as lack of agency.

But that's not how life works. When institutions are sick, they just stop working and it leaves a profound sense of betrayal. People become disoriented. Things always worked before, they think, even if they don't know how. Someone made sure that the lights went on and the water kept running. But what we're seeing is that fewer and fewer people know how to make things work. We've been conditioned to believe that a nameless, faceless "they" keep the essentials of life flowing while the smart, creative people figure out how to enrich themselves with the golden crumbs of an affluent society. After the Colonial Pipeline was hacked and shut down for a few days in 2021, the CEO said it was possible to operate the pipeline on a more or less manual basis by running some workarounds on the automated systems, but the people who knew how to do it had mostly retired or died.

The implosion of the Fyre Festival and the scandals of WeWork and Theranos weren't just bad deals. They reflect a system of incentives and a public morality that encourage aiming for the big payout as fast as possible, even if it requires cutting corners or deceiving investors and customers. If it all goes bust, you can still get paid and stick the public with the bill, like the banks did in 2008, and if you're clever, like Neumann at WeWork, you can walk away without ever paying a price, and even be grossly enriched with investor money. It's every man for himself—no accountability, no sustainability, no reality except the quick buck.

When institutions exercise something close to monopoly power, their constituents become their captives. Even when they are meant to serve the public, with no profit calculation, they may lose sight of their mission and operate primarily for the benefit of those who run them. The public education system is a familiar example. From 1950 to 2009, the number of teachers grew 2.5 times as much as the student population, while the number of administrators grew 7 times as much.[14] Students today are not 7 times better educated than they were in 1950; they're not 2.5 times better educated either. By pretty much any metric, recent graduates from American high schools know less on average than did graduates in 1950.

Just as primary and secondary schools too often prioritize staff over students, or the institution over its constituents, colleges and universities are geared to sustain themselves first, regardless of value to students. Faculty members trying to secure tenure are unlikely to challenge the system or ask whether a college degree is worth the cost. Candidates for a PhD are unlikely to spend much time wondering if they were accepted into the program so the graduate faculty can justify its existence. The system overproduces aspirants to professorships, and the stiff competition for tenured positions makes it imprudent to challenge the status quo.

A central imperative of academic competition is to publish or perish, and one result is that much of what gets published is of dubious value. It's easy to ridicule much that comes out of the humanities, but in the sciences a different kind of credibility problem has emerged. Scientists have found that a large number of studies cannot be replicated to confirm the accuracy of their findings. This means that the original results are questionable at best, and sometimes simply false. A survey of nearly 1,600 research scientists by *Nature* in 2016 found that "more than 70% of researchers have tried and failed to reproduce another scientist's experiments and more than half have failed to reproduce their own experiments."[15] One of the first people to call attention to the replication crisis was John Ioannidis, an early public skeptic of Theranos.

Gwern Branwen, a brilliant and enigmatic researcher, identifies numerous reasons why so many scientific studies cannot be replicated:

> The crisis is caused by methods & publishing procedures which interpret random noise as important results, far too small datasets, selective analysis by an analyst trying to reach expected/desired results, publication bias, poor implementation of existing best-practices, nontrivial levels of research fraud, software errors, philosophical beliefs among researchers that false positives are acceptable, neglect of known confounding like genetics, and skewed incentives (financial & professional) to publish "hot" results.

With so many sources of inaccuracy, "any individual piece of research typically establishes little. Scientific validation comes not from small *p*-values, but from discovering a regular feature of the world which disinterested third parties can discover with straightforward research done independently on new data with new procedures—*replication*." Unfortunately, writes Branwen, "seriously mistaken statistics combined with poor incentives has led to masses of misleading research" in many fields, not only social sciences but also areas of genetics (principally candidate-gene research), biomedical science, and biology in general.[16]

This is a problem in a time when the very name of science is so ostentatiously revered. Presentist hubris is predicated on the belief that we have been set free from irrational beliefs and fears—a proposition that is unfalsifiable, since whatever is irrational must be deemed unscientific. The term "science" is so fetishized that many nonscientific fields of study have adopted "science" as part of their name in order to appropriate its credibility. Think of fields like social science, political science, or management science.

We expect science to reveal the definitive, objective truth, but many decisions in public policy, medical practice, and other areas have been based on scientific studies that turned out to be misleading. For example, Pfizer got FDA approval for Vioxx in 1999 on the basis of studies later shown to be deeply flawed. An estimated 140,000 people suffered coronary heart disease and approximately 60,000 died as a result of taking Vioxx before it was pulled from the market in 2004. The Sackler family's Purdue Pharmaceutical used bogus "science" to persuade doctors to prescribe OxyContin for just about anything more painful than a hangnail, which precipitated an ongoing epidemic of opioid addiction that has so far afflicted millions and killed hundreds of thousands. These cases amounted to betrayal of the people who trusted their doctor and the FDA.

Despite the many examples of failure or even outright fraud, many people continue to hold anything labeled "science" in uncritically high regard. People make decisions based on "the science" without consideration of "the common sense," and without looking for flaws, errors, or omissions. By deferring to "science," one can effectively pass the buck and shift responsibility onto an amorphous nonentity rather than a person. And that's the basis on which public officials make policy that effects the lives of many millions. Should we quarantine the healthy rather than the sick as was done with Covid? What constitutes a healthy diet? What causes the climate to change? What kind of research should be subsidized? Is industrial-scale, monoculture farming a boon because it lowers the price of food, or is it bad because it destroys topsoil and relies heavily on carcinogenic chemicals? The result is that we make bad decisions, with predictably bad outcomes. And there are no real professional penalties for what is often clear malpractice.

For years now there has been less science as a joyful voyage of discovery and more bland, paper-pushing careerism. It gives off an air of confined exhaustion. And it's the institutions and the incentives they create that form the cage.

Universities often seem better at advancing revolution than at advancing knowledge. Nonsensical and destructive ideas spread rapidly through the institution because of social pressure to line up behind the latest hysterias and radical demands—or get in front of the revolution before it consumes you. Institutional leaders tend to find that the most comfortable course is to go along with it all.

A few years ago, college administrators determined that their campuses were so unsafe that they had to install blue-light emergency telephones. Like mushrooms, the phones began appearing on campuses across the country. If you've been on a college campus lately you've seen them. But this puts the colleges in an odd position. Their progressive faculty and student groups had demanded action to make students "feel safe" from what they claimed was a rape epidemic, among other threats. At the same time, administrators needed to convince parents to send their children to live on those campuses. I've witnessed parents asking campus tour guides, "Why do you have so many of these emergency phones on your campus? Is this a violent place?" To which the flummoxed guide responds—honestly—that the campus is quite safe, in fact, but isn't it great that precautions have been taken nonetheless. It would have been pointless for administrators to dispute the premise behind installing these emergency phones: one does not reason with a mob.

Those who run American universities understand their role as being the vanguard of a never-ending revolution that is constantly remaking the culture, rather than preserving and nurturing the culture and transmitting it to the next generation. When sensemaking institutions are doing their job right, they explain what it means to be a valuable, fully integrated part of the society, and they provide a framework in which people can live productive, dignified lives and prepare the next generation to do the same. Everyone needs to know who they are and where they fit in, and sensemaking institutions provide answers to those questions. But many of our dominant institutions—academia, media, government, large corporations—have placed themselves in opposition to the family and the church, which are the permanent institutions of human life because they are part of the created order. This opposition drives many of the social conflicts and pathologies that afflict our country.

When sensemaking institutions don't reinforce the nation's culture and are at odds with the permanent features of life, they create a conflict for those with strong families and an active faith. But for people without them, it creates a vacuum which places them in a situation in which they must invent personal narratives so they can frame their lives. The theory is that this is good because it represents personal liberation. In reality, it dissolves social bonds and increases isolation. This is not liberation, it's degradation. About one-third of Americans report that they are lonely.[17] And loneliness is one of the leading reasons that people seek counseling—essentially paying someone to talk to them. The CDC reports that social isolation—an extreme form of loneliness—is linked to significantly increased risk of dementia and of premature death—perhaps as high as that associated with smoking or obesity.[18]

Nature can be denied but it cannot be overturned. Human beings are necessarily interdependent, but when people are encouraged to think of themselves primarily as individuals whose highest purpose is to maximize personal happiness, it's harder for them to be part of a church or a family or to be a good neighbor. Marriages become transactional, and all too often ephemeral or nonexistent. *What are you doing for me?* becomes the normative question, not *How do we build a family together?* Employers see workers as a means of production. It becomes the true war of all against all. This has been called weaponized interdependence, in which reliance on others turns into exploitation. The term has most often been used to describe the ill effects of globalization, but the concept applies to social and institutional relations as well. No nation can sustain itself that way.

Escaping from the tyranny of weaponized interdependence does not mean ending interdependence. If escaping meant radical independence, that would be too much and would fail. Even desiring that sort of escape is just a sort of defeatist reaction to the fact that the relationships and institutions that are supposed to be pro-social and edifying are instead malfunctioning and malignant. But the libertarian fantasy doesn't work as a model for a stable society. Some forms of breaking free from institutions can be helpful instrumentally, to minimize the power of misbehaving gatekeepers. Later I will discuss how cryptocurrency and a decentralized internet, for example, can help create space to rebuild strong institutions that support a healthy, vital culture.

Weaponized interdependence will end only when the sense makers recover their purpose and commit to a common-good interdependence that favors family, faith, and culture, or when they are replaced by others that do. There will always be a ruling class, or elites who control dominant institutions, and people who naturally seek status and power. In the best scenario, their status and success will be tied to national success. Developing elites and sensemaking, status-granting institutions that are both morally and materially committed to the nation is central to the project of restoring cultural vitality.

Looking at the sclerotic self-indulgence of America's once vital institutions, it's easy to see a bleak, overdetermined future of ongoing and inevitable decline. The Roman Empire is often evoked as the classic precedent, which produces a sense of American hysteresis—of self-reinforcing decline and failure, suggesting a similar destiny for America. While the hysteresis is real, it's continuance is not inevitable. That's too fatalistic, and it doesn't take account of Rome's ups and downs, its periods of glory, decay, crisis, and revitalization. It also gives too little credit to human agency. The years leading up to Julius Caesar's ascension to power and becoming the adoptive father of Augustus, the future emperor, were marked by civil and political strife, which intensified into civil war after his assassination. It would have been easy to see nothing but continuing decay in Rome's future. But Augustus won uncontested control of the empire and set about reversing the trajectory, leading Rome to new heights. Later on, poor leadership in combination with external pressures brought more troubles, particularly in the third-century imperial crisis. Then a restoration of order followed, for a time, with Diocletian's administrative reforms.

Nothing is foreordained. The actions of a capable and determined few make a difference.

4

THE POLITICS
OF DECAY

EVERY REGIME MAKES CERTAIN PROMISES TO ITS PEOPLE, and a mismatch between those promises and the observable reality creates a problem. Modern democracy is premised upon sustained economic growth, which itself is predicated upon technological progress. It's an essential part of how we see ourselves, how we set our expectations, and how we plan our lives. The lack of real, long-term growth creates a set of challenges that modern societies including America are ill-equipped to address and that threaten political stability.

The explicit promise of modern democracy is equality as the basis for the rule of law, a transparent political process for making decisions (such as elections and legislative procedures), and a protected set of fundamental rights. It should be noted, however, that the definition of equality is contested and colors every modern political question in some way, especially the question of what rights are fundamental enough to require protection by the state. Second, the rule of law is not unique to modern liberal democracies. What's unique is that modern democratic regimes base their claim to legitimacy at least in part on their ability to protect a set of rights, whereas legitimacy in the premodern world was based on duties to kin, community, and God or gods. Another way to frame the difference is that modern democracies promise happiness or at least the right to pursue it, whereas premodern societies offered glory, honor, and immortality through one's children, tribe, and faith.

The promise of happiness has come to be largely equated with material prosperity. The expectation of increasing prosperity is basic to how we understand ourselves as a nation and how we as individuals plan our lives—and increasing prosperity depends on growth. The lack of real, long-term growth thus presents a challenge for the American regime and could undermine the political stability we have taken for granted.

To people who have grown up in liberal societies, it may seem false and even immoral to say that democratic equality depends on economic growth. Political conservatives tend to understand liberal democracy largely as a product of moral will, a result of virtuous people apprehending the natural rights of man through either reason or revelation and then establishing a political regime centered on the defense of those rights. That is basically the conservative understanding of the American founding, and also the predicate for American involvement in regime-change efforts abroad. Left-liberals generally understand modern democracy as the result of historical forces that make it both right and inevitable—which is essentially a form of historical determinism. Both views have elements to commend them, but both are overly theoretical and fail to take full account of the material and cultural contexts in which liberal democracy developed and where it has been most successful.

We can start in the seventeenth century with the English Civil War, which was a bridge between the premodern and the modern world. The struggle between Crown and Parliament presaged the American War of Independence and the French Revolution. Political changes throughout Europe followed in the nineteenth century, especially the 1848 revolutions and their aftermath. Then came the final destruction of the Prussian, Italian, Russian, and Hapsburg monarchies in the early twentieth century. The few monarchies that survived became powerless testaments to past glory.

What is too often overlooked is the extent to which this political development coincided with two centuries of rapid and continuous improvement in the material conditions of life, beginning a few decades before the founding of the American republic. This was a period unique in human history: at no other time have the living standards of ordinary people risen so much, so consistently, for so long. It was the result of sustained technological progress that dramatically increased productivity and generated unprecedented material abundance, which was more broadly distributed than the wealth of earlier golden ages. That sustained progress ended around 1960, which the influential blogger Scott Alexander has called "the year the singularity was cancelled." The long period of robust innovation came to a close half a century ago. There is still innovation, of course, but it is concentrated in certain areas, especially information technology, and doesn't deliver the same broad-based prosperity as before.

Some will counter that global growth has continued. But it is primarily what economists call catch-up growth, which is simply the economic growth that occurs as the result of developing countries adopting the innovations that raised living standards in the West. China is the clearest example of catch-up growth. It is not the same as growth coming from new innovations.

When innovation slows, productivity growth slows, and when productivity growth slows, so does growth in living standards. Since about 1970, American living standards in the aggregate have improved very slowly at best, and for many people they have started to decline. More and more households now require two incomes to make ends meet. By some economic measures, those two incomes and the consumption that goes with them would register as a better standard of living, but the overall trend toward two-income households is a symptom of slower growth.

At the same time, a slow-growth or no-growth economy sets up the conditions for a massive concentration of wealth in a few hands, to a degree previously unknown in America. A small number of individuals and mega-corporations have amassed riches and economic power far in excess of what the large trusts in oil, railroads, and steel possessed before they were broken up in the early twentieth century. The magnitude of wealth concentration we see today can lead to destabilizing social conflict.

There are ways to mitigate this danger, but the remedies that have the most political support right now don't solve the problem and would have harmful consequences. An attempt to redistribute wealth on a large scale would be socially and economically destructive and would intensify long-simmering political conflicts. High taxes—whether on income or estates or wealth—would not solve the fundamental problem of stagnant growth and would most likely exacerbate it. And since large corporations and the wealthiest citizens have historically had no problem calling in political favors to game the tax system, higher tax rates are likely to increase social and political polarization.

Our society was built on promises that effectively presuppose the sort of growth that has not existed in decades. Because people have set their expectations based on those promises, stagnation is experienced not just as unfulfilled expectations but also as broken promises. The mismatch between the promises made by the regime and the reality of what it can deliver leads to social unrest and political decay. If the mismatch cannot be remedied, it must be rationalized in some way, or else another unifying force is needed to legitimize the political and social order. This could be religion, or it could be a sense of civilizational destiny or national glory, but material prosperity is never enough, and when it declines or disappears, something else is required.

The American regime as designed by the Founders, codified in the Constitution, and implemented after ratification is a republic. It is a system in which the people, through the mediating institutions of the states and the Electoral College, choose a chief executive, the president. He is not a monarch, but it's useful to think of the president as a temporary monarch. Remember that George Washington was offered that job but he declined.

Historically, monarchs often made themselves champions of the common people against an ambitious aristocracy. The American system doesn't have a formal aristocracy, of course, but it's inevitable that a few will have considerably more wealth and power than the many, as in every country. The president is allied with the people who elected him and is expected to protect their mutual interests. The alliance between monarchy and democracy in the American system has the same goal as alliances between the king and the people have always had: to thwart the ambitions of the oligarchy.

You might be thinking: "We don't have an aristocracy. We're America!" But every society has something like an aristocratic elite. There are differences in how much power they wield, and whether their exercise of power is open or hidden. In the United States, the elites and their institutions obscure their power with misdirection—*This is a middle-class nation!*—or a meticulously maintained veneer of benevolence: *We are doing what is wise and for your benefit. Trust us.*

It wasn't always this way. Early America was essentially a middle-class nation consisting mostly of self-sustaining families engaged in agriculture or small-scale crafts and trade. There was no heavy concentration of wealth until the twentieth century. More importantly, there was the promise of social mobility—the chance of moving up the ladder through ability, effort, and providence. This was partly a result of our social and political structures, and partly a consequence of our history as a frontier nation, where free land acted as a massive economic subsidy and a spiritual boost, expanding visions of the possible. It was that mobility that acted as the essential American social lubricant, tempering envy and keeping faith in self-government alive.

Abraham Lincoln articulated the American ideal of social mobility, and the dignity of rising from a lowly condition, in his State of the Union Address in 1861. He also expressed a particularly American view of the relationship between labor and capital, a subject that was very much on people's minds as the country industrialized, and in the wake of the 1848 revolts in Europe. There was no necessity for "the free hired laborer being fixed to that condition for life," Lincoln said.

Many independent men everywhere in these States a few years back in their lives were hired laborers. The prudent, penniless beginner in the world labors for wages awhile, saves a surplus with which to buy tools or land for himself, then labors on his own account another while, and at length hires another new beginner to help him. This is the just and generous and prosperous system which opens the way to all, gives hope to all, and consequent energy and progress and im-provement of condition to all. No men living are more worthy to be trusted than those who toil up from poverty; none less inclined to take or touch aught which they have not honestly earned.

Lincoln warned that the freedom to rise higher could be lost without vigilance: "Let them beware of surrendering a political power which they already possess, and which if surrendered will surely be used to close the door of advancement against such as they and to fix new disabilities and burdens upon them till all of liberty shall be lost."

Lincoln had been speaking publicly about the subject of mobility for several years by the time he attained the presidency. He envisioned a nation where ingenuity, industry, and prudence would allow a pauper to become a merchant prince, or at least achieve some measure of financial independence. And he explicitly linked that economic independence to political independence and cultural vitality. The ideal he described was a reality to a large extent in antebellum America, particularly in the North.

The idea of social mobility is still central to the American national identity. We love the story of the hardworking kid from the wrong side of the tracks who makes good. The somewhat darker corollary is that we like it just as much when the rich and powerful are brought tumbling back to earth by foolishness, sloth, or even just bad luck. Yet popular resentment of the wealthy and powerful has been kept minimal by the belief that people are not locked into a particular social station. Unlike the people of many older countries, Americans generally like to see others get ahead, or at least they don't resent it, because they think it's possible for anyone to get ahead with hard work and a little luck. And if they don't quite strike it rich, they are confident that the average person can lead a decent, dignified life and support a family.

The nineteenth century was generally an age of rapid growth across the board, especially after the Civil War resolved the political crises that had roiled America for the preceding decades. The country was growing by just about every relevant metric: raw land mass, states entering the Union, industrial and agricultural production, and technological advances. New universities were being established across the country. At the personal level, families were growing and life expectancy was increasing. It was a golden age. The country was healthy, vital, and peaceful.

The period between 1900 and 1920 was the first time that a significant concentration of wealth occurred in America. It was also a time of concentrating power in the federal government. The early American regime was one where governmental action was exercised primarily at the state or local level, in accordance with the constitutional design. The twentieth century brought a rapid centralization of power, starting in the Progressive Era, accelerating with the New Deal, and never stopping until it reached the logical limit of what was possible with the technology and resources at the federal government's disposal.

That centralization created a new social class that is functionally an oligarchy. James Burnham described part of it as the professional managerial class or "managerial elite." Those are the people of the modern oligarchy. Its central institutions are universities and the media. They are the status-granting, sensemaking institutions that set the goals and define the boundaries of acceptable thought and action. The adjacent institutions with political and economic power are primarily instrumental, implementing the agenda and enforcing the values defined by universities and media. Those institutions include the permanent bureaucracy, the judiciary, NGOs, and large corporations, which increasingly are controlled not by their founders, CEOs, or operating executives, but by Human Resources, Legal, and ESG (Environmental, Social, and Governance) departments. Most ambitious people aspire to membership in these institutions.

Michael Lind explained how the activities of these various institutions, public and private, are essentially coordinated—if not formally, then through a similarity of background and outlook among the people who lead them:

> The private, public, and nonprofit sectors in modern developed nations do not have separate and distinct elites that can be counted upon to check each other. Instead, the private sector tends to dominate the public sector through campaign finance, and the nonprofit sector through donations. Even in the absence of these methods of elite coordination, the fact that almost all of the personnel of elite institutions of all kinds belong to the managerial-professional class and have similar educations and shared outlooks produces a common mentality, tending toward Orwellian groupthink among corporate executives, investment bankers, elected politicians, civil servants, and nonprofit leaders. Managerial dominance is reinforced by lateral mobility at the top levels of society. Diplomats become investment bankers, investment bankers become ambassadors, generals sit on corporate boards, and corporate executives sit on nonprofit boards.[1]

Note the reference to "lateral mobility" between branches of the managerial elite, as distinct from the vertical mobility that was previously the hallmark of American society.

Like any country, the United States needs smart, educated, energetic people who take on big responsibilities, in positions where they can actually do good. If they appear to be public-spirited, the general public will not resent their prominence. But the oligarchic managerial class has failed in its central responsibilities to the nation. The period in which the managerial elite has been ascendant, the past half century, has also been the period in which American innovation has largely stalled, productivity growth slowed to a crawl, real wages for the middle and lower class stagnated, wealth concentrated at the very top, social conflict increased, fertility collapsed, chronic disease became endemic and, in recent years, life expectancy declined. The reasons for the failure of elites are partly spiritual or moral, reflecting a lack of personal and civic virtue; partly ideological, the result of false or misleading ideas about human nature and society; and partly a response to material conditions brought about by secular cycles. Determining the right proportions of blame is a fool's errand. What's more important is identifying actions that can remedy this failure, which I will discuss later.

The period between 1900 and 1920 was the first time that a significant concentration of wealth occurred in America. As large fortunes began to accumulate in the United States in the early twentieth century and a sizable urban underclass started to form, there was a spike in "instability events," such as riots and terrorism, exceeding even the 1860s, as shown in the graph below. But subsequently the promise and reality of social mobil-

FIGURE SIX

Frequency of Instability Events Every Five Years Since 1780

Source: Peter Turchin, "Dynamics of political instability in the United States, 1780–2010," *Journal of Peace Research* 49:4 (2012).

ity largely kept the peace, even as newly wealthy industrialists consolidated their position. The era directly following World War II was mostly stable; in fact, the first decade after the war had the lowest incidence of instability events since the 1840s.

This was also a time of impressive technological innovation, culminating with the Apollo space program (1961–1972). In a way, the Apollo program was a highly institutionalized replay of the wartime Manhattan Project. Both were major leaps forward, with unintended knock-on effects. The Manhattan Project resulted in something truly new in a very short time, but also made science in America a ward of the state, with stultifying consequences. The Apollo program built upon existing rocket technology, though the size, scope, and audacity of the project to send men to the moon—which was laudable—necessitated the development of various new technologies that were later widely adopted.

When Apollo 11 landed on the moon on July 20, 1969, it was a triumph—and the high-water mark of an era. Indeed, all the markers of social, political, cultural, and economic health were at or near their secular peaks. Less than three weeks later, on the night of August 8–9, Sharon Tate and four others were murdered by members of the Manson Family. The nation was shocked. Then, a week later, on August 15, Woodstock began in Upstate New York. The long ascendancy of the Baby Boomers was inaugurated. It was the passing from one age to another and it included a blood sacrifice.[2]

After Apollo, technological progress slowed down except in limited areas, particularly computing and information technology, leading to the unprecedented wealth accumulation of the tech titans. We tend to think that disparities of wealth were more extreme in the premodern past, but some historical comparisons show this is a false assumption.

In the early fourteenth century, the richest man in England was the Earl of Lancaster, with annual income of £11,000, which was about 5,000 times that of a skilled mason. In early seventeenth-century France, the richest man was Armand-Jean du Plessis, the cardinal and duke of Richelieu, who became the powerful first minister of France. Richelieu's annual income has been estimated at several million livres. Ordinary workers in France lived on roughly a hundred livres per year, so the cardinal's income was perhaps 20,000 times that of a Parisian working man. We might easily view that kind of economic disparity as outrageous, and congratulate ourselves on our greater egalitarianism. But should we?

It's hard to compare today's mega-rich with their historical counterparts because they don't have much ordinary income; their wealth is tied to financial assets, usually equity in a large company. America's richest man, Jeff Bezos, doesn't take a salary, but from 2019 to 2020 the value of his holdings in Amazon rose by something like $60 billion. Median annual income for an American worker was a bit less than $53,000 in 2020.[3] Bezos increased his wealth by 1,132,075 times the median income.

Perhaps that's an unfair comparison because Amazon stock had a very good year. Bill Gates, who founded Microsoft but has sold or donated most of his shares in the company, possesses a fortune recently estimated to exceed $130 billion. It's reasonable to say that Gates could earn a 5 percent return on that holding, which amounts to $6.5 billion per year. That's 122,641 times the median income. Even a mere 1 percent return would be 25,528 times the median income. In other words, the most conservative calculation of income for America's second richest man is far richer compared to the average American than Richelieu was to the average Frenchman.

History shows that violent uprisings often follow a period of extreme wealth accumulation by a small group that is not shared by the many in some tangible way. For much of its history, America avoided this fate. National wealth grew quickly, fortunes were made, but there was still a large, vibrant, prosperous middle class. This prevented the sort of resentment that leads to conflict. But that's no longer the case. Could it be that America is courting revolution? The idea may seem outlandish, but in our relatively short history we've had a civil war, a big spike in political instability events such as riots and terrorism in 1919–1920, and a smaller spike in the 1960s. The increasing concentration of wealth and power in fewer hands makes America more vulnerable to some triggering event that could precipitate factional conflict, then mass violence, and possibly state failure. We are vulnerable in part because we don't realize it.

I want to stress that inequality in income and wealth is natural in human society, arising from differences in intelligence, sociability, attractiveness, health, family, and many other things including fortune. The fact of inequality per se is not wrong. In some ways we even want to encourage it. The drive for excellence, for victory, for mastery in a particular domain is an essential feature of human life and can bring benefits to the wider society. It is not wealth and income disparities per se that cause instability. Rather, extreme economic disparity in combination with a lack of social mobility is what breeds a sense of injustice, frustration, and conflict. Wealth is a rough measure of social status and recognition, which are fundamental human motivators. There are other ways that societies confer recognition. Premodern societies were often more concerned with glory and honor than gold. We remember Achilles but not the merchant who had the Myrmidons' victual contract. But in our society, recognition is most easily conferred and measured by wealth.

When wealth is heavily concentrated and when stagnation impedes mobility at the same time, social decay follows and often leads to conflict. Social cohesion erodes when it seems impossible for the middle class to get ahead, and equally impossible for the upper class to fail.

In recent decades, social mobility has been decreasing in America. The children of the rich tend to stay rich. For simplicity's sake, we'll say "the rich" are the top 0.1 percent of the income ladder, though a superwealthy elite of a few hundred families are really in a class of their own. The wastrel may turn a $50 million trust fund into $25 million but remains rich. The children of the upper middle class likewise tend to remain in that class throughout their lives. Assortative mating reinforces the social stratification. Those in the broad middle class, which for my purposes includes what others call the working class, are not moving up but are increasingly proletarianized, as I described earlier.

FIGURE SEVEN

Inheritance of Income Status

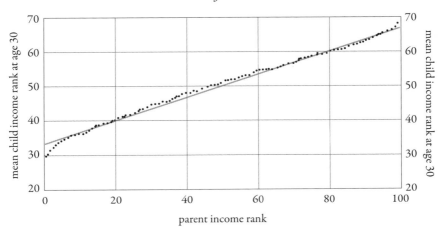

Source: Raj Chetty et al., "Where is the Land of Opportunity? The Geography of Intergenerational Mobility in the United States," *Quarterly Journal of Economics* 129:4 (2014).

Raj Chetty, an economist at Harvard, found a remarkably high correlation of income status between a 1980–82 birth cohort at age thirty and their parents at the same age, as shown in the graph above.[4] Chetty and his colleagues also found that social mobility has declined for every birth cohort since 1940. Whereas 90 percent of those born in 1940 earned more than their parents at age thirty, the same was true for only 50 percent of those born in the 1980s. A decline in absolute mobility was seen in all fifty states, but it was especially steep in states of the industrial Midwest such as Michigan and Illinois, where the rates went from 95 percent for people born in 1940 to 41 percent for those born in 1984.[5]

As an explanation for the collapse of social mobility, Chetty points to slower GDP growth and a more unequal distribution of the gains from growth. But why have the gains been distributed so unevenly? Elsewhere Chetty identifies family structure, education, and the example set by peer families as important variables for social mobility. Those are plausible factors, but history demonstrates that slow growth in itself leads to a more unequal distribution of wealth. One of the most important reasons for this is the relationship between capital and labor. When labor is plentiful, it is cheap, and excess returns accumulate to capital. When labor is in short supply, wages are higher. Robust growth brings more demand for labor, and therefore rising wages.

Over the past fifty or so years, two trends greatly increased the size of the labor force in the United States and globally. The first was the large-scale entrance of women into the workforce, beginning in earnest in the 1970s. The labor force participation rate of women was 37.7 in 1960; the figure was 56.2 percent in 2020. Over the same period, the labor force participation rate for men fell from 83.3 percent to 67.7 percent. Together these trends were approaching something like equilibrium, but China was then emerging into the global market as a virtually bottomless well of cheap labor. Advances in transportation, logistics capabilities, and communications enabled easy access to Chinese labor and large-scale distribution of China's manufactured goods. China is still adding numbers to the global manufacturing labor force.

Corporate power in the United States has been consolidating, so every major industry is now controlled by a handful of market-dominant players. A relatively small number of employers have more control of the labor market and more bargaining power over employees than in the past. Finding a better deal is more likely to require moving to another part of the country, which breaks social bonds and detaches people from the extended families that can provide not just love and friendship but an organic safety net. The social order is made less stable.

While these trends were underway, most of the gains in real wages were being captured by those at the top of the income distribution. Between 1978 and 2018, real wages rose 37.6 percent for those in the 90th income percentile, 6.1 percent for those in the 50th percentile, and a scant 1.6 percent for those in the 10th percentile.[6] In annual terms, the gains for those in the 90th percentile—the cut-off for the upper middle class—were only about 0.8 percent. The gains were much bigger for those in the top 1 percent, and even more so for the small fraction at the very top. And this is just looking at income, to say nothing of wealth accumulation.

Real Wage Trends, 1979–2018, by Selected Demographic Characteristics

Demographic	Real wage trends	Cumulative change in real wages		
		10th percentile	*50th percentile*	*90th percentile*
Overall	90th percentile	1.6%	6.1%	37.6%
	50th percentile			
	10th percentile			

Shaded bars = recessions

Source: Congressional Research Service, "Real Wage Trends, 1979 to 2019," R45090.

For those in the 50th percentile, the gains were effectively nothing. At the same time, the cost of purchasing the things that historically have been considered hallmarks of middle-class life increased at a faster rate. These include higher education, health care, and housing, especially in places where well-paid jobs are clustered. The cost of being middle-class keeps rising and squeezing people out. Those who manage to stay middle-class have to work harder at it.

"Middle class" in America no longer means the stability of owning a home that gets paid off in your fifties or sixties, a secure retirement income that will make ends meet, and same or better for your kids. Rather, it means being reliant on two household incomes instead of one, credit card debt, a home equity loan, refinancing your mortgage in your forties and restarting the thirty-year clock to freedom, and getting a reverse mortgage in your seventies or eighties to meet the expenses that Social Security and savings won't cover. Median household retirement savings for those 55–64 years old in 2020 was $134,000—not nearly enough for a secure retirement. Nearly half had no retirement savings at all.[7] Most of the people in that group are defined as Baby Boomers, a generation that has done better than the subsequent generations. And it's easy to slip out of the middle class and into the underclass, whether through bad luck or bad behavior.

The main path upward for the middle class has been through academic credentials—usually college and increasingly a graduate degree. In 1970, about 11 percent of American adults had a college degree. In 2019, the figure was about 36 percent.[8] Over the same time, the median real income for college graduates dropped from $58,350 to $50,219.[9] Meanwhile, the cost of higher education in a public institution increased by a factor of about 3.5 in real terms.[10] As a consequence, 69 percent of students now graduate with college debt averaging $29,900.[11] This is a picture of precarity developing into downward mobility.

There is pressure on people higher up the ladder too as wealth concentrates at the top while gains diminish at every level below. The biggest fortunes today dwarf those of a few decades ago in constant dollars. In 1985, the richest man in America was Sam Walton, the founder of Wal-Mart. *Forbes* estimated that he was worth $2.82 billion—the equivalent of $6.77 billion in 2020 dollars. The net worth of Jeff Bezos is more than twenty times that sum. It now takes a lot more money to be rich—and to be upper-middle-class too. There is competition to keep up throughout the elite ecosystem and among elite-aspirants, who are mostly either the children of the professional upper middle class or those who aspire to it and get a taste of it through an elite or semi-elite education.

One way that elite-aspirants try to distinguish themselves and climb upward is by getting a degree from one of a small number of top universities. A Harvard degree is well known to be a reliable entry pass into elite circles, and the competition to get one has escalated. The number of freshmen admitted to Harvard each year has remained essentially the same for decades while the number of applicants has soared. The admission rate in 1985 was 16 percent. In 2020 it was only 5.2 percent.

In the hope of gaining an advantage over the multitudes with bachelor's degrees, many elite-aspirants seek a graduate degree of some kind. A law degree has long been a way for smart, ambitious people to gain a secure place in the upper middle class, but an overproduction of lawyers changes the equation. In 1970 there were 326,000 lawyers in the United States, which worked out to 1.59 for every 1,000 Americans.[12] By 2019 there were 1,352,000 lawyers, or 4.1 per 1,000. The median income for lawyers dropped over that time, while litigiousness soared. It's been a lose-lose proposition for individuals and for the country.

Doctoral degrees are somewhat less associated with wealth, but still a status marker. Candidates sacrifice a number of income-earning years to get the degree, but in many fields there are far more PhDs graduated each year than there are tenure-track faculty positions open. This is especially true in the humanities, but even in the hard sciences there's an overproduction of doctoral degrees. Though science PhDs are much more employable outside academia at something approximating the compensation and status they expect, there are diminishing returns even here.

Elite-aspirants who get the credentials may find themselves in a fierce contest for a limited set of high-status positions. At a given time there are only five hundred CEOs in the S&P 500, only one editor of the *New York Times*, only fifty governors, only a hundred senators, only one president, and so on. The competition for every elite position or status marker—every credential, every job, every office, every honor or award—is intense. Many elite-aspirants will be disappointed.

When elite-aspirants are overproduced, the result is a restless group of talented, ambitious people with frustrated expectations. They generally have enough resources to exercise some agency, but are not free from economic concerns. They can be a volatile class. As wealth, power, and status are concentrated in fewer hands, there are more people who feel deprived of what is justly theirs. This feeling can spark intra-elite conflict, which historically has been a prime vector of societal instability—more dangerous to social order than popular unrest in the face of unified elites.

Great concentrations of wealth are commonly thought to provoke revolutions from below—uprisings of downtrodden peasants or proletarians with nothing to lose but their chains. There's some truth to this, as there have been many rebellions of peasants or urban poor, especially starting in the late Middle Ages in Europe, and in other parts of the world too. But peasant uprisings have typically been crushed easily, without accomplishing permanent reform. Popular rebellions typically lack internal cohesion, a clear sense of purpose, and the expertise to govern or affect policy and build staying power. Elite factions are more likely to have those assets, which is why intra-elite conflicts are more dangerous. As they grow in intensity, the lower classes are compelled to align with one faction or another.

Jack Goldstone describes the competition for status and wealth in seventeenth-century England as one in which "Limits on available land, civil and ecclesiastical offices, and royal patronage led to increasingly polarized factional battles between patron-client groups for available spoils."[13] This factional competition would play into the rebellion of Parliament against the Crown, in which aristocrats could be found on both sides of the conflict.

Peter Turchin argues that "declining economic fortunes of aristocrats create the climate conducive to interpersonal and interfactional conflict." But he also notes that "the purely materialistic calculation—'I lack sufficient funds to support the lifestyle to which I am entitled by birth, and I will obtain this money by force if necessary'—is just one possible motive driving violence, and not necessarily the most powerful." A materialistic motive may be paramount to some people, while for others, the moralists, it is only a small part of what precipitates action. "When an aristocratic faction…monopolizes all largesse flowing from the state, they offend not only against the pocketbook of those excluded, but also against their moral feeling. It is not fair, it is not right that a small clique is rolling in luxury while everybody else suffers. The moralistic impulse is to punish the offender." The moralists, seeking to rectify injustice, organize themselves into action groups. "Such faction formation is the usual stage before the full-blown revolution," Turchin observes.[14]

The history of France in the seventeenth century is instructive. Richelieu died in 1642 and was replaced by Cardinal Mazarin, whose ability to amass fantastic wealth for himself and his supporters dwarfed even Richelieu's. In 1648, France fell into a civil war known as the Fronde when a faction of nobles rebelled against the monarchy, at one point forcing the king to flee Paris with his family. The king's party triumphed in 1653, setting the stage for the absolute monarchy of Louis XIV and his descendants who would rule until the Revolution in 1789. Because he restored order after an extended period of turmoil, absolutist or not, Louis XIV was popular and established the legitimacy of strong French monarchs for the next century. That monarchy, however, came to be seen mostly as the guardian of unjust privilege. The French Revolution was in part an uprising of the poor against the wealthy nobility, but also a rebellion of a rising, restless, and atheistic bourgeoisie.

The other great modern revolution, the Russian Revolution, wasn't a popular revolution at all. It was a putsch by dispossessed and ambitious intellectuals and elite-aspirants, supported by elements of the aristocracy that had simply lost faith in their right and, more importantly, their capacity to rule. The Bolsheviks were not an organic movement of the working class, of the peasants, of the small farmers. In fact, they infamously despised the kulaks—a class of small farmers that emerged after the czar emancipated the serfs in the nineteenth century—and regarded them as reactionaries loyal to the old regime. Lenin called them bloodsuckers and Stalin ordered that they "be liquidated as a class," leading to millions of deaths. Nor was Lenin a proletarian Spartacus, but an ambitious intellectual from a wealthy family. The same was true of Leon Trotsky's family, who were prosperous farmers. Both were younger sons whose prospects were pinched despite their families' wealth.

Any nation is on dangerous ground when people like Lenin and Trotsky—smart, educated, from successful families—find little hope for a better future, or come to believe they will be worse off than their parents. That is one reason why the decline of economic mobility in the United States is concerning.

The slowdown of innovation and growth not only accelerated a concentration of wealth at the top, but also put stress on the condominium that was established between the two major political parties after the war. In

1985, Mikhail Gorbachev initiated the liberalization program known as glasnost, and a few years later, in 1989, the Soviet Union disintegrated. The United States was left, for a time, as the world's sole superpower and hegemon.

America had already committed itself to a form of internationalism—what would come to be called globalism—that would accelerate the disintegrative structural and demographic forces that have brought us to the present crisis. In reality, the postwar American project of both major political parties was exporting American liberalism and its institutions abroad, not simply defeating or even containing Soviet expansionism or communist ideological imperialism. This can be found as early as the Atlantic Charter of 1940, which might be called the founding document of the postwar international order. The agenda of spreading liberal democracy and subservience to the U.S.-dominated system of international organizations and NGOs—by force when necessary—around the world continued after the Soviet Union disintegrated in 1989.

Even now that sounds pretty attractive to American ears. But not so much as it did before 2003, the year we invaded Iraq. That's because the burdens of empire are heavy. What was once understood as defeating communist expansion and helping the developing world catch up in economic growth underwent enormous mission creep and turned into the multidecade, serial disaster of "nation building" in places like Afghanistan, Iraq, Yemen, and Somalia, to say nothing of "regime change" operations in Ukraine and a failed attempt in Venezuela. Our empire of anti-imperialism failed at great cost to America and Americans.

Alongside the nation-building projects came a push for across-the-board expansion of international trade. It had two purposes during the Cold War: The first was to strengthen and deepen the ties that bound together the anticommunist world, the better to present a united front against the Soviet bloc. The second was to make war less likely. Similarly, an explicit purpose of the European Union is to render war between European nations nearly impossible. These were admirable aims, and appropriate to the time. Expanding trade between Europe and the United States, and among European countries, was largely beneficial.

The United States, mostly untouched by the ravages of the world wars, enjoyed industrial dominance for a few decades, but Europe rebuilt and the European Union reached a rough parity with the United States as an economic power. European policy on issues like labor unions, work safety rules, and environmental regulation is similar to that of the United States, though there are some differences—as there are between the prosperous countries of northwestern Europe and the less prosperous ones in the south.

But as the Cold War drew to a close, the goalposts moved. What had been a policy of increased trade between equals evolved into a policy of global free trade. This meant that American companies paying wages sufficient for an American lifestyle and subject to American safety and environmental regulations had to compete with Chinese companies hiring former peasants at a pittance and operating under far less regulation. It was a sharply tilted playing field. The post facto rationalizations were as stupid as they were cruel: American workers were lazy and should learn to compete in a global economy; American companies needed to innovate faster; free trade is good in the aggregate. But American workers weren't lazy. It was just that they couldn't possibly compete with workers whose wages were at least 75 percent lower. And the main innovation that American companies made to address the problem was to move operations to China and other low-wage countries and fire their American employees. For some time, the middle and professional classes were insulated from the harm of globalization, but the economic pressure has crept up the social ladder as even their jobs have been outsourced, or lost to workers imported on visas to experience something like indentured servitude to employers.

Both political parties contributed to this situation. The parties have had policy differences, to be sure, but each has promoted a variation on a common theme and developed a particular framing of the project and its own distinct policies, but always within the same framework. One of those themes has been that price declines are always beneficial. But this means that labor costs must decline. Making lower costs the moral imperative of economic life meant that labor—and with it, manufacturing—had to be moved offshore to the cheapest provider. That was done without regard to its effect on the people left unemployed or underemployed, to the long-term prosperity of the country, to national security, to the ability to innovate, or even to basic self-sufficiency in critical goods. Many Americans were surprised to discover in 2020 that the United States does not produce any of the most common antibiotics, nor any of the chemical precursors required for their production.

Both parties have needed to respond to the material reality developing around them and to mounting public anxiety about fading social and economic prospects. Starting in the 1960s, the Republican Party was the party of libertarian economics and market solutions for just about everything. Some of those solutions made sense, such as tax breaks for savings for education and health care. But other policies had truly harmful consequences. One example is the Financial Services Modernization Act of 1999, which repealed the Glass-Steagall regulations enacted after the Great Depression. The policy was first promoted by Republicans, with the support of libertarian economists, though the resulting law passed the Senate 90-8 and the House 362-57 before being signed by a Democratic president, Bill Clinton. It allowed commercial banks to own investment banks and insurance companies and to engage in proprietary trading. This was supposed to let banks grow big enough to be competitive with the large foreign banks, which sounded good at the time. But one outcome was a massive consolidation in banking and black-box institutions, creating systemic financial risk. And as we saw in the period from 2005 to 2010, the size of the institutions led not only to regulatory capture but to national capture: the banks could privatize their profits and socialize their losses because Wells Fargo or Citibank or Chase could take the nonfinancial economy down with them if they weren't permitted to unload their losses on the Federal Reserve.

From the 1980s until 2016, all of the policy and rhetoric from Republicans was directed at lowering wages to make American companies "more competitive with foreign competition." The problem was that it was never possible to drive wages low enough to compete with Chinese labor. By the 1990s, Democrats had largely conceded the point, and with Treasury secretaries like Robert Rubin under Clinton and Larry Summers under Obama, it became the party of Wall Street, financialization, and deindustrialization. It is now the party of the coasts, the big cities, the very wealthy, the large corporate interests including Big Tech, the professional managerial class and those who aspire to it, along with those who are dependent on government assistance and recent immigrants. That coalition leads mainstream Democrats to support mass immigration, which gives the corporate part of their coalition cheap labor while simultaneously producing new voters beholden to the party.

The core constituency of the Republican Party has also changed. It is now the party of interior America and the wage-earning middle and working classes. People who had been "neglected, ignored, and abandoned" elected Donald Trump in 2016 because he promised to bring back manufacturing jobs, start a massive national infrastructure program, raise wages, and protect their interests. Not since 1956, when Dwight Eisenhower ran on raising the minimum wage and expanding Social Security and unemployment insurance, had a Republican presidential candidate talked about the desirability of rising wages.

It's certainly not the first time that major party realignment has happened, or at least been attempted. In the 1920s, a group of intellectuals who came to be called Neo-Tories saw Britain in trouble. The trenches had consumed the flower of a generation. Many old families were on the brink of extinction, having lost an only son and suffering economic hardship. The Irish question weighed heavy. The nature of the empire was unclear and the mother country's grasp on it was tenuous. And the working classes were anxious. World War I, after all, came at the crest of the last great wave of globalization. The Neo-Tories' critique of democracy will sound familiar to modern ears.

William Sanderson, a leading Neo-Tory thinker, observed that democracy always "tends to divide nations into two classes with hostile interests—a small plutocratic or bureaucratic minority which rules, and the whole body of the people who must obey." While noting that the United States was "ruled by millionaires," he also said: "Democracy means, and has always meant, government by middle-class intellectuals," while socialism, especially in its Fabian form, "is merely a tendency towards the establishment of the power of middle-class bureaucrats," especially because the Labour Party "has for reasons best known to itself chosen middle-class intellectuals as leaders."[15]

Sanderson's description sounds familiar in light of the present relationship between the superwealthy and the managerial class who run the nation's sensemaking and status-granting institutions and staff the upper levels of the federal bureaucracy. There is some friction between those two groups over how wealth, power, and status are distributed. But the bigger gap is between those two groups that collectively have captured a disproportionate share of the available wealth, power, and status, on the one hand, and everyone else. This divide has been described in various ways, though a good shorthand for the conflict is the one coined by my late friend Angelo Codevilla, who described it as the ruling class versus the country class. This distinction avoids both ideological and party labels, which would miss important aspects of the structural tensions that act as political stressors and are sublimated into party politics. The tension between the ruling class and the country class is profound, but often obscured by ruling-class factional conflicts, for which the country class is dragooned into action as unwitting foot soldiers who lose no matter which faction wins.

Those are the politics of stagnation, which are really the politics of decay. Slower technological progress means lower economic growth, stalling social mobility, and greater concentrations of wealth and power at the top. Factional conflict increases, weakening the political order. A triggering event could then lead to widespread violence and even a regime collapse. The stakes could not be higher.

There is no neutral: if the path is not forward, then it is backward. The need for solutions is urgent, especially as global challengers grow more assertive.

5

AMERICA IN THE WORLD

THE TWENTIETH CENTURY WAS UNDOUBTEDLY THE AMERICAN century, but that wasn't clear at the outset. Great Britain still ruled an empire on which the sun never set, and led the world in commerce. France was prosperous and secure, with her own overseas colonies, and was regarded as the world's cultural capital in the Belle Époque. This was also the first great era of globalization, and the rivalries it stirred up ended in war. America's industrial might, along with a decisive role in determining the outcome of World War I, secured her place among the great powers.

At the beginning of the twenty-first century, America's role in the world looked as secure as Britain's had seemed a century before. The Cold War was won, a peace dividend was being spent, and liberalism appeared to be spreading around the world. The End of History was declared. American economists, consultants, and agencies like USAID spent the 1990s showing former communist countries how to run their governments and economies the American way. It would be a sort of Marshall Plan 2.0.

And that was the problem. Solutions devised for the challenges of another time and place were updated with a bit of monetarism here and some public choice economics there. They were then promoted with far too much self-congratulation and too little understanding of the contexts in which they were being applied. A nation's history, culture, religion, folkways, even its geography were largely ignored.

America's foreign policy since 1945 has rested on a belief that the future of all countries should be a variant of American liberalism and that America's role in the world is to bring that future into being. The collapse of the Soviet Union seemed to confirm the correctness of this mission, but it led to a dangerous hubris. America has been crusading around the world, using our military to remake it in our image—engaging in wars, military interventions, coups, and color revolutions far and wide, with diminishing success and compounding cost. All this has sapped the national vitality. The messianic conception of America's role in the world is a product of twentieth-century conditions and is at odds with the historic American idea. President James Monroe succinctly described America's historic conception of itself and its place in the world:

> Our policy in regard to Europe, which was adopted at an early stage of the wars which have so long agitated that quarter of the globe, nevertheless remains the same, which is, not to interfere in the internal concerns of any of its powers; to consider the government de facto as the legitimate government for us; to cultivate friendly relations with it, and to preserve those relations by a frank, firm, and manly policy, meeting in all instances the just claims of every power, submitting to injuries from none.

America's recent understanding of its place in the world has also come into growing friction with the self-understanding of other nations. Five key events that occurred around the turn of the twenty-first century signaled trajectories diverging from American expectations for a liberal world order of nation-states.

1) January 1, 1999: The euro was formally introduced as the common

currency of the European Union. This was a major step in consolidating a common European identity and building an economic powerhouse that would come to rival the United States.

2) December 31, 1999: Vladimir Putin was appointed acting president of the Russian Federation, and a few months later he was elected to that office. The stage had been set for Putin's rise to power after Anatoly Chubais—the golden boy of Western reformers—devalued the ruble at the insistence of American economists, breaking the economy and impoverishing nearly everyone in Russia except the gangsters and oligarchs who became the new ruling class.

3) September 11, 2001: The United States suffered a series of terror attacks that shook up the conventional thinking about nation-state conflict. The resulting wars in Afghanistan, Iraq, and Syria lasted for more than two decades and are not entirely in the past.

4) December 11, 2001: China became a member of the World Trade Organization, giving a great boost to China's economic power and its ambition to remake the world order around Chinese priorities.

5) March 14, 2003: Recep Tayyip Erdoğan became prime minister of Turkey, an office he held until 2014, when he became president. He remains in that position as head of an explicitly Islamic party but also a populist and nationalist one. Erdoğan's central aim is to assert Turkish distinctness from the West.

Each of these events marks an inflection point for the major powers now vying for position in a multipolar world. Just as America took her place among the great European powers a century ago, so there is a new order emerging, but the jostling for preeminence is different from the global dynamic we've been accustomed to. Apart from the United States, the main players today are best understood as civilization-states rather than nation-states, the latter concept being in part a construct of Western liberalism. A common theme in the emerging global order is reasserting national sovereignty, cultural independence, and civilizational identity, while decoupling from the West (or the United States). This is not to say that the major powers are necessarily at odds with the United States or each other, but they are often eager to distinguish themselves from Western liberalism, to reclaim their own traditions and forge ahead on their own terms. Europe, for its part, aims to shake off the status of vassal of the American imperium it has held since 1945 and chart a more independent course, diverging by just a degree or two at first, but more so over time. The European Union is a means of doing so.

Russia has explicitly rejected the Western path. "The liberal idea has become obsolete," Putin said in 2019. "It has come into conflict with the interests of the overwhelming majority of the population."[1] Russia is modeling itself on its own unique form, quite distinct from modern liberalism. The Russian Orthodox Church has been restored to a place of honor, and it is growing. Cathedrals and church buildings seized by the communists have been reconsecrated. "We are experiencing the second baptism of Russia," said Andrei Kormukhin, a leader of an organization that supports the Orthodox Church.[2] "We are going to the real true values: family, church, and state," declared Vitaly Milonov, a lawmaker of the United Russia party.[3]

Vladimir Putin is used in the West as a rhetorical bogeyman, a stand-in for everything that good people are supposed to oppose. But that is at least in part because Putin and his project, seen through the lens of American liberalism, are misunderstood, and Russia, the great Eurasian power, is easy to portray as the dangerous other. But just as we want to be clear-eyed about our own interests, we must be at pains to understand others as they understand themselves.

Putin is quite clear about his goals and how he sees Russia's place in the world. In a speech to the Valdai Club in 2013, he said that Russia "has always evolved as a state-civilisation, reinforced by the Russian people, Russian language, Russian culture, Russian Orthodox Church and the country's other traditional religions. It is precisely the state-civilisation model that has shaped our state polity." Speaking to the Russian Federal Assembly in 2012, Putin said, "We must value the unique experience passed on to us by our forefathers. For centuries, Russia developed as a multiethnic nation (from the very beginning), a state-civilisation bonded by the Russian people, Russian language and Russian culture native for all of us, uniting us and preventing us from dissolving in this diverse world."[4]

The American national security establishment was surprised when Russia invaded Ukraine in February 2022. They shouldn't have been. Vladimir Putin and influential Russian intellectuals have been very clear about the threats they see to Russian civilization. To the experts' surprise was added chagrin at the response of much of the world to U.S. attempts to ostracize Russia. Europe and the Anglosphere generally did Washington's bidding. But China, India, and many of the Gulf states deepened their ties to Russia and increased bilateral trade even as the United States was implementing a sweeping sanctions regime. What's most challenging for America is China, which has used America's proxy war on Russia to hasten global dedollarization and position itself as a leader in the emerging multipolar world.

Like Russia, China is best understood as a civilization-state. Westerners often see it mostly in economic terms, as a "developing economy" and a trading partner. This is narrowly true, but it misses a lot. Alternatively, China is viewed ideologically, as a communist country run by doctrinaire Marxists and a successor to the Soviet Union in Cold War 2.0. Americans should wish it were so, because it would make for a much less potent rival. Instead, like Russia, it is a civilization-state that draws on its civilizational history as a foundation for global preeminence.

In his book *The China Wave: Rise of a Civilizational State*, Zhang Weiwei emphasized that history and how it informs a holistic view of society:

China is now the only country in the world which has amalgamated the world's longest continuous civilization with a huge modern state.... Being the world's longest continuous civilization has allowed China's traditions to evolve, develop and adapt in virtually all branches of human knowledge and practices, such as political governance, economics, education, art, music, literature, architecture, military, sports, food and medicine. The original, continuous and endogenous nature of these traditions is indeed rare and unique in the world.[5]

Zhang observed that historical events had turned other parts of the world away from the path of developing into civilization-states:

[I]f the ancient Roman empire had not disintegrated and been able to accomplish the transformation into a modern state, then today's Europe could also be a medium-sized civilizational state; if the Islamic world today made up of dozens of countries could become unified under one modern governing regime, it could also be a civilizational state with more than a billion people, but the chance for all these scenarios has long gone, and in the world today, China is the sole country where the world's longest continuous civilization and a modern state are merged into one.[6]

China is not without its challenges. But it is also full of both latent and realized power. When China joined the WTO in 2001, the assumption in Washington was that the Chinese were signing up for the same program that had been in force for decades: America rules through a system of institutions created in the 1940s and 1950s to embody a rules-based international order. Everyone gets something, but it's essentially an American regime. Others can dance, but the United States calls the tune. China had a different plan: *We'll join, but we're running our own program and building toward the day when we're in charge.*

Tian Feilong, a law professor in Beijing, explained the prevailing Chinese attitude this way: "Back when I was weak, I had to totally play by your rules. Now I'm strong and have confidence, so why can't I lay down my own rules and values and ideas?" He continued: "Sorry, the goal now is not Westernization; it's the great rejuvenation of the Chinese nation."[7]

China's leaders are smart and serious, and their resolve to pursue a distinctively Chinese future is supported by a powerful critique of the West. One of the foremost theorists of Chinese state power, Jiang Shigong, described what he saw as the fatal weaknesses of the American-dominated world order:

> [The current state of world empire] faces three great unsolvable problems: the ever-increasing inequality created by the liberal economy; state failure, political decline, and ineffective governance caused by political liberalism; and decadence and nihilism created by cultural liberalism. In the face of these difficulties, even the United States has pulled back in terms of worldwide military strategy, which means that world empire 1.0 is currently facing a great crisis, and that revolts, resistance, and revolution from within the empire are unravelling the system.[8]

The world is presently multipolar, with ancient empires reemerging as civilization-states vying for either global or regional power: China, India, Turkey, and Europe. In the Chinese view, the world naturally has a single hegemon, and maybe that is right. Perhaps there must be one power that defines and enforces the global order. It's a self-serving position for the Chinese to take, since only two powers could fill that role in the foreseeable future: the United States as the incumbent, or China, the large, rich, unified, ambitious rising power. Europe cannot possibly take on this role and doesn't seem to want it. The other powers are too small. The Chinese believe their destiny is to replace the American hegemon.

China, Russia, and the other powers contesting U.S. hegemony present critiques of American liberalism that are often withering. They assert that what America offers isn't worth having, and that other visions of the future are deeper, more satisfying, and better suited to their own people. While

American liberalism emphasizes procedural neutrality in the service of individual autonomy, the civilization-states offer unity and purpose. Emmanuel Macron, the president of France, gave a perceptive speech in 2019 noting the strengths he saw in the major civilization-states: "Take India, Russia and China for example. They have a lot more political inspiration than Europeans today. They take a logical approach to the world, they have a genuine philosophy, a resourcefulness that we have to a certain extent lost."[9] Macron made the case for a pan-European civilization-state that he described as a "humanist project" with roots in the Enlightenment. He also urged his audience to "listen to the discourse in Hungary or Russia." While the European project he envisions could not be advanced by Catholic Hungary or Orthodox Russia, he observed that those countries "have a cultural, civilizational vitality that is inspiring."[10]

France of course has its own civilization, related by history to those nearby yet distinct from them. France existed long before its current governing structure, the Fifth Republic. It is a civilization with a state, related to but distinct from nearby civilizations. The French Revolution was a political fork in the history of that civilization, but the old culture persists in tension with the post-Enlightenment regime. French Catholics, for example, have continued to be among the most faithful in Europe, even as their numbers have shrunk in the officially secular republic. Likewise, France maintains a devotion to high culture—wine, haute cuisine, fashion, art, music, and artisanal crafts—that is the envy of the world.

In America too there is internal conflict over our national identity. Is it still rooted in the pre-Enlightenment, Christian nation inaugurated in the early 1600s and established over the following 150 years that gained its independence in 1783 and then adopted the representative political system established by the Constitution? Or is it a project based on Enlightenment humanism begun in 1776 and then formalized in 1789? The conflict between these two conceptions is present throughout American politics.

This leaves America with a challenge because we do not understand ourselves as a civilization-state. The dominant American self-understanding today is highly idealized and dependent upon an ideological view of the world that separates man into different components: religious, political, private, public, and so forth. This is basically the humanist project that Macron describes. It can be viewed two ways: the better version is that it's a modus vivendi allowing people with different and competing faiths to live and work together; the other version is that it's an intentional war on faith itself or at least that the practical effect is to degrade and suppress religion.

Either way, the civilization-states are presenting a competing vision of life, politics, culture—of civilization itself—that poses a challenge we are not presently equipped to answer substantively. On its current path, the United States is likely to become less powerful in relative terms as technology developed here and in other advanced countries becomes more widely distributed. It will take a major breakthrough in science for America's lead in wealth and the power that comes with it to begin growing again.

Over the near future, China and the United States will compete for global dominance while the smaller civilization-states vie for regional supremacy and tack between the larger powers. This is a multilayered global environment that American statesmen have not seen before, and navigating it will require wisdom and caution. Mistakes that we could afford to make as the undisputed hegemon will carry a much higher cost.

While the challenge from China is widely acknowledged, the nature of that challenge is not what is generally believed. One popular theory is that we are heading into a "Thucydides Trap" in which the risks of war between the rising power and the incumbent hegemon are dangerously increasing to the point of making war inevitable, just as Thucydides described the dynamics between Athens and Sparta in the lead-up to the Peloponnesian War. American policymakers frame relations with China as something like another Cold War and call for new carrier battlegroups to patrol the western Pacific. This idea rests on a fundamental misunderstanding of what is happening, and of American interests and capabilities.

The United States and China are far less likely to become embroiled in direct military conflict than were the United States and the Soviet Union when they had scores of divisions facing each other in Central Europe. Slightly more possible though still unlikely would be proxy wars akin to those fought in places like Angola, Mozambique, Vietnam, Nicaragua, and El Salvador during the Cold War. And for all the tough talk about Hong Kong, the Senkaku Islands, and Taiwan, does anyone seriously think the United States would, could, or should send hundreds of thousands of troops across the Pacific to defend their borders when we don't protect our own?

An important difference between China today and the old Soviet Union is economic. In 1980, the Soviet economy was about 40 percent the size of the American economy. China's economy is now at parity with that of the United States by some measures and will almost certainly surpass it in the not-too-distant future. That economic threat is primarily one of America's own creation. China would have risen as an economic power in any case, but American policy for many years favored China and encouraged actions by American companies that undermined domestic industry, at great cost to interior America.

China's leaders know that military confrontation with the United States would be a poor choice strategically and would not serve their long-term goals. As Xi Jinping explained, "The path of peaceful development is the Party's strategic choice, in line with the times and aligned with the fundamental interests of the country."[11] This strategy may not hold forever. But for now, the Chinese recognize that they are still a developing nation, which can best exert and increase its power through shrewd policy and economic leverage to reshape the global system in favor of Chinese interests.

In 2015, Xi issued a directive ordering a "holistic" approach to national security, placing "ideological security," "economic security," and "cultural security" on par with military concerns.[12] The concern for "ideological security" is not surprising since the state is run by the Chinese Communist Party, which describes itself as Leninist but pursues a distinctively Chinese form of socialism. Every regime, including the American one, aims to defend and promote its legitimizing myths and ideas. But the concern for "cultural security" is the mark of a civilization, not just a state. In fact, the Chinese state regards itself as the steward of a civilization with a unique and valued culture. Guarding and sustaining that culture is seen as essential to the nation's future well-being.

The challenge from China is not military; it is economic, cultural, and political. China's size and success present the world with an alternative to America as the global hegemon. Manfred Weber, the leader of the European People's Party in the European Parliament, recognizes that China poses a cultural challenge to Europe as well. "China is a system competitor who challenges the values of the EU," he said. Weber added that the EU's economic response should be one that affirms and protects those values: "Therefore, modern trade policy must be linked to our principles."[13]

There is broad agreement that the current world order cannot last. Anne-Marie Slaughter, former director of policy planning at the State Department, rightly said at a roundtable for Chatham House in 2020 that we "aren't going to run the world in 2045 [with] the institutions created in 1945."[14] There is much less agreement on what will or should replace them. Thinking about a different future is hard for Americans since we built the existing order, but the worst possible course would be to let it slip away without proactively shaping a new one that serves our needs.

The Chinese subscribe to a materialist theory of history, in which the material productive forces of the age proceed independently of human will. They also believe that China is riding those forces into global supremacy. In the Western view of history, human choice and initiative make a difference. We can and must act to influence the global future in our interest. All of human experience says that it does and it is on that basis that we must act.

It is possible that America could simply recede on the global stage while China replaces it as the head of a unipolar world run by the Chinese Communist Party. That's unlikely for a number of reasons, and it couldn't happen unless America allowed it. Another scenario is a world in which the institutions of the old order—such as the UN, the WTO, and NATO—decline in power and influence, and the civilization-states exist in a truly multipolar world of regional hegemonies and shifting bilateral and multilateral alignments. That would look something like European Great Power politics on a larger scale.

The best future would be one in which America leads a bloc supporting national sovereignty and cooperation between a diverse group of civilization-states and smaller powers that wish to maintain their particular traditions, cultures, and institutions against the homogenizing forces of globalism. This bloc would recognize both the benefits and the perils of globalization—the movement of people, goods, capital, and ideas across borders and around the world. Technology makes such movement impossible to reverse even if that were desirable, but peoples and nations must be allowed to manage it as they judge best. American policy can serve Americans—and the people of other nations—by leading a rollback of the globalist tide.

Today the American hegemon is increasingly viewed abroad as "an anti-civilisation, dissolving the variety of European and other cultures in the harsh solvent of global capital."[15] This description bites because there is a recognizable element of truth in it. In the globalist order, nongovernmental organizations (funded either privately or with public money), very large corporations, and aligned governments work together for their mutual benefit, but often in ways that conflict with the interests and expressed desires of the people of sovereign nations. It is a supranational system with very little transparency or accountability.

The telos of the globalist order is purely materialist. In that sense it is the apotheosis of modern liberalism, which views man as a walking stomach. This is apparent in Marxism but there is a similar understanding present in Austrian economics. The Austrians have the better of the argument with Marx and are much closer to the truth about human nature, but both see man primarily as a collection of appetites. They mistake a part for the whole.

Man has a stomach that must be fed, but that is not the whole man, and the important function of nourishing the body is only a part of man's purpose.

Reducing man to *Homo economicus* is deeply unsatisfying because it's a denial of reality. As Alexandre Kojève noted, the worker—the anonymous cog in the economic machine—will (*must*, in his telling) demand recognition. This can be seen in today's identity politics, where an ever-multiplying variety of intersectionally combined and recombined identities are arrayed against each other, creating a system of politically and culturally unsustainable rivalries.

America must remember this as we seek to restore our vitality and show the way forward. Attending to the material aspects of life is important, but material concerns must be ordered toward some unifying and worthwhile end. First, our society must be reordered to protect and nurture the prepolitical human institutions of human life—family, church, and friendship—that give life its meaning and provide it with depth and sweetness. A revitalizing project should also encourage the qualities degraded by materialist culture: duty, loyalty, grace, and beauty, among others. We cannot allow our politics—and therefore our nation—to be a contest between communism and plutocracy.

We also need to recover the dynamism that fuels productive innovation. We're not there now, partially as a result of a decadent drift, but partly by design. Our society prioritizes status over excellence and innovation. Too much energy goes into destructive rivalry. In itself, competition for status is natural to humanity. One of the hallmarks of a successful civilization is its ability to reduce unproductive status competition and channel those energies into productive endeavors. Without a sense of purpose and responsibility, too much human activity reduces to mere status seeking, which is especially pronounced during periods of absolute or relative scarcity or stagnation, when the situation is perceived as zero-sum.

America has been the architect and leading exponent of the globalist order. America can now lead in replacing it with an order that is less homogenizing, more respectful of traditional cultures and social structures, and more favorable to human flourishing. We should aim for an order that is elevating rather than flattening. This effort must begin at home.

One common question asked in politics today is, "What to do about China?" But that's not quite the right framing of the question concerning the global challenges ahead. It rests on an assumption that if we "do something about China," or any other rival, it will be good for America. If we stop their rise, we can maintain the status quo at home. But this amounts to a kind of managed decline. The right question is, "What to do about America?" Our best policy is to focus on what strengthens America, what makes us more secure, more unified, more dynamic, and better able to sustain ourselves independently in the future. We can start by looking at the characteristics of exceptionally creative and productive societies in the past.

6

GOLDEN AGES
AND THE ROOTS
OF VITALITY

"HISTORY IS MADE BY ACTIVE, DETERMINED MINORITIES, NOT BY the majority, which seldom has a clear and consistent idea of what it really wants," wrote Ted Kaczynski. He was right about that. For good or ill, the ambition and resolve of a few can be highly consequential. In American political history one need only look at the Founders. Breaking from the mother country was not a majority cause when the Declaration of Independence was signed. This is often true with revolutions. The Bolsheviks were hardly a majority party, but Lenin's determination and lack of scruples enabled him, along with a small, dedicated cadre, to work his will upon Russia and change the course of global history. Looking back further, we can identify many times when small numbers of people have exercised a disproportionate influence on civilization.

Consider the Golden Age of ancient Greece, when there were perhaps 250,000–300,000 people in Attica, the region that includes Athens. The number of adult male citizens was around 60,000 at the start of the Peloponnesian War in 431 BC. The other Greek city-states were much smaller. Corinth, one of the larger cities, had perhaps 15,000 adult male citizens. By modern standards the Hellenic world was quite small. And out of that small population there was a yet smaller subset of highly generative people who were responsible for an amazing amount of discovery that would improve people's lives as the new knowledge was distributed worldwide. Over the period of a few hundred years the Greeks effectively created philosophy, revolutionized mathematics, laid the foundations of geometry, discovered the spherical earth, and invented the truss roof,[1] the winch, the foundations of geometry, and the spiral staircase. They built the first known railway at Diolkos, near Corinth, around 600 BC. The first central heating system was installed in the Temple of Artemis near Ephesus around 350 BC. This is nowhere near a comprehensive list of Greek accomplishments.

Invention is sometimes the result of intense focus born of necessity, as when there is an existential threat. It might originate from a wish to make practical tasks more efficient. But often it grows out of a desire to reach higher, do better, and probe the bounds of possibility. The Greeks called it *thymos*, a drive to rise above the common lot and achieve distinction. "Thymos is the side of man that deliberately seeks out struggle and sacrifice, that tries to prove that the self is something better and higher than a fearful, needy, instinctual, physically determined animal," as Francis Fukuyama explained it. "Not all men feel this pull, but for those who do, thymos cannot be satisfied by the knowledge that they are merely equal in worth to all other human beings." This impulse fuels achievements in many domains—art, music, science, technology, even politics. It is a normal part of human nature, though it has flourished more strikingly in some cultures than others, at particular times and places.

Everyone acknowledges the great burst of creativity that occurred in Italy and especially in Florence beginning in the fourteenth century, but many people who study innovation and productivity aren't quite sure how to measure what happened there. The Italian Renaissance occurred during the Little Ice Age, which began around 1300 and depressed agricultural production, causing intermittent famine. The devastating Black Death hit

Europe during the early years of the Renaissance. Conflict was frequent among the Italian states. In the fifteenth century, agricultural production increased and population rebounded. Florence's urban population is estimated to have peaked at 70,000 in 1526, another plague year, before declining again.[2]

Italy, like ancient Greece, was mostly composed of small city-states, which led Europe in commercial development, generating wealth to patronize artists. Culturally, Italy became in some ways the center of the world, and Florence was its beating heart. Consider that Leonardo da Vinci, Michelangelo, and Machiavelli all lived and worked there at the same time. A remarkable number of outstanding artists and scholars were born in Florence or nearby, including Giotto (who pioneered a more naturalistic painting style), Boccaccio, Filippo Brunelleschi, Lorenzo Ghiberti, Donatello, Fra Angelico (born in Fiesole), Masaccio, Filippo Lippi, Benozzo Gozzoli, Botticelli, Domenico Ghirlandaio, Machiavelli, and Benvenuto Cellini. Brunelleschi led the way in developing a Renaissance school of architecture, most famously designing the dome of the city's cathedral. Among the artists drawn to Florence from other towns were Raphael, Leonardo da Vinci, and Michelangelo. Artists flourished under the patronage of the Medici and other wealthy families, while civic organizations commissioned public art.

The Florentine money-lending trade effectively created the foundation for modern banking, and with it capitalism and the commercial class. One example of the influence this Florentine innovation had on Europe is in the person of Thomas Cromwell, the chief minister to Henry VIII and leading architect of Tudor power. After fighting as a French mercenary at the Battle of Garigliano in 1503, Cromwell had found himself in Florence, where he entered into the service of Francesco Frescobaldi, a prominent banker. He returned to England with knowledge of the banking trade as well as useful contacts, which he applied with his native intelligence and initiative to put Henry's financial house in order.

Two centuries later, the foundations for the Industrial Revolution were laid in northern England, following upon an agricultural revolution that increased productivity. The epicenter of innovation in manufacturing was the county of Lancashire, where the largest city was Manchester. It counted about 25,000 inhabitants in 1773, but the population soon grew rapidly, to 95,000 in 1802.[3] This was a consequence of developments that began in 1733 with John Kay's invention of the flying shuttle, which doubled the productivity of weavers. James Hargreaves, also of Lancashire, developed the spinning jenny in 1764. Five years later another Lancastrian, Richard Arkwright, patented his revolutionary water frame, which used cylinders rather than the operator's fingers to twist thread and could spin many threads simultaneously without skilled labor. On this basis, Arkwright created the modern factory system. With the addition of James Watt's steam engine (1775) and Edmund Cartwright's power loom (1785), productivity increased by a factor of forty and the English textile industry took off. In 1750, it used 2.5 million pounds of raw cotton; in 1800, the quantity was 52 million pounds; in 1850, it was 588 million.[4]

The inventions of Watt and Arkwright were applied far beyond textile manufacture. In combination with advances in metallurgy, they gave rise to the steel industry. Major innovations were made in chemicals, machine tools, and transportation—first canals, then turnpikes and railroads—chemicals, and machine tools. England became an industrial powerhouse.

The population of England was not especially large—approximately 7.5 million in 1780—of which perhaps one-third were adult males or 2.5 million. Again, this is quite a small population by modern standards yet the country generated a disproportionate amount of scientific and technological progress in a fairly short period of time. Nearly all of this innovation happened not in London, the nation's metropolis with its population of around a million, but in smaller towns and cities far from the capital. Those inventions and discoveries would contribute to lifting standards of living worldwide.

Meanwhile, the great intellectual ferment known as the Scottish Enlightenment was going on a little to the north, in the modest city of Edinburgh, population about 80,000 in the later eighteenth century. Over the period of a few decades, Edinburgh was home to Francis Hutcheson and David Hume, both distinguished philosophers; Adam Smith, the father of modern economics; James Hutton, the founder of modern geology; Joseph Black, the physician, physicist, and chemist who discovered magnesium, carbon dioxide, and the concept of specific heat; John Playfair, a mathematician; and the poet Robert Burns.

The Scottish Enlightenment was the work of a few dozen people, most of whom knew each other. Many socialized together and some developed long-term friendships. Hutton, for example, was friends with Smith, Playfair, and Hume. They built a culture of collaboration and competition that was institutionally centered at the University of Edinburgh, though much of the activity went on at private social clubs, the Select Society and its successor, the Poker Club, where recreation was combined with intellectual stimulation. Hume described how an evening at the Poker Club could clear his mind of fruitless speculations: "Most fortunately it happens that since reason is incapable of dispelling these clouds, nature herself suffices to that purpose. ... I dine, I play a game of backgammon, I converse, and am merry with my friends; and when after three or four hours amusement, I return to these speculations, they appear so cold, and strain'd, and ridiculous, that I cannot find it in my heart to enter into them any farther."[5] Through their social relationships, people with similar interests inspired one another and often competed. As iron sharpens iron, the proverb goes, so one man sharpens another.

A century later, fin-de-siècle Vienna was a place where numerous eminent artists and intellectuals knew and influenced each other, including Gustav Klimt and Egon Schiele in visuals arts, Gustav Mahler in music, and Otto Wagner in architecture—to name just a few. Ludwig Wittgenstein was born into a very wealthy Viennese family, and as a young man he used some of his inheritance to underwrite promising artists and writers in the city, though most of his own career was spent in Berlin and later teaching at Cambridge. The great Kunsthistorisches Museum of Vienna opened in 1891. Among the many distinguished people who lived in the city, Sigmund Freud was the most famous and his work, for good or ill, had the broadest and most lasting impact on the world, as his theories essentially gave birth to the modern therapeutic state.

Each of these examples was, for a time, effectively the main engine for human creativity and defined an era. Another kind of creative flowering was concentrated in the Santa Clara Valley of California in the later twentieth century. It began when Robert Noyce invented the monolithic integrated circuit at Fairchild Semiconductor, a company he had cofounded two years earlier. His invention was made of silicon, inspiring the nickname Silicon Valley. In 1968, together with Gordon Moore, Noyce founded Intel Corporation, where they oversaw the development of the microprocessor. This was the revolution in atoms that was the necessary predicate for the revolution in bits—the software and internet technology that have reshaped our daily routines over the past few decades. Moore has his own law: the number of transistors in a dense integrated circuit will double roughly every two years.

A storied rank of technology companies began springing up in Silicon Valley. Fairchild Semiconductor and Xerox Corporation's legendary Palo Alto Research Center (PARC) were foundational. Then came the likes of Atari (1972), Apple (1976), Oracle (1977), Sun Microsystems (1982, now part of Oracle), Adobe (1982), Electronic Arts (1982), Cisco Systems (1984), Yahoo! (1994), Netflix (1997), PayPal (1998), Google (1998, now Alphabet), Salesforce (1999), Tesla (2003), Twitter (2006), and Square (2009). Mark Zuckerberg famously started Facebook in 2004 while he was at Harvard, but a few months later he relocated to Palo Alto, where his company got its first venture investment from Peter Thiel and grew into the giant it is today, now called Meta.

The Silicon Valley tech culture has been partly fed by Stanford University, which Bill Hewlett and David Packard attended before starting the Hewlett-Packard Company in a Palo Alto garage in 1939. Besides PARC, the area is home to research facilities related to the military. But much of Santa Clara County has nothing to do with the tech industry. I'll use six towns to represent the heart of Silicon Valley: Palo Alto (home of Stanford), Mountain View, Sunnyvale, Menlo Park, Atherton, and Cupertino. In 1970 they had a combined population of a bit over 250,000. In 1980 it was still only around 288,000. Forty years later, in 2020, a little more than 400,000 people lived in those cities. While San Jose and Redwood City and some other towns in the vicinity are also part of the Silicon Valley ecosystem, the core has always been the area immediately around Stanford. The north side of the campus is bordered by Sand Hill Road, famous as the location of many of the world's most storied and successful venture capital firms.

The driving force of the recent tech revolution, especially in the golden era from the founding of Intel in 1968 up to the late 1990s, was a relatively small community of likeminded people in Silicon Valley working on basically the same project: making the world a better place with computer technology, first atoms and then bits. It was a remarkably productive group of people much like those who created the Industrial Revolution in northern England in the late eighteenth century. Silicon Valley is still generative today, though there is a sense even among the people who live there that innovation has slowed down.

The energy of Silicon Valley has attracted many people with similar ambitions, but tech companies still seek out more people with particular skills and aptitudes. How to find them? In one famous example, in 2004, Google placed white billboards near Harvard Square and by freeways in Silicon Valley bearing a cryptic message: "*{first 10-digit prime found in consecutive digits of e}.com*." It's a math riddle, and it was enticing to a certain type of person. Those who solved it found themselves on a website presenting a more complex math problem. If they solved the second problem, they were led to a webpage that invited them to submit a résumé to

Google. There's a certain appeal to the idea of a community of brilliant nerds building the future. That vision, the drive, the execution, and the pursuit of excellence are all highly charismatic.

A small community dedicated to a particular project and inspired by an idea of excellence can be highly productive, but first come the individuals who simply enjoy the process of invention. Silicon Valley was founded by dilettantes, not careerists. Today, *dilettante* is synonymous with *dabbler*, but I mean it in the older sense of an amateur who delights in something. The word derives from the Latin *delectare*. From Hewlett and Packard tinkering in their garage, to Mark Zuckerberg coding in his dorm room, people motivated by the joy of discovery, or delight in accomplishing something that had never been done, have pushed technical frontiers. The same holds true for someone like Palmer Luckey, the homeschooled creator of the Oculus virtual reality headset that he sold to Facebook for $3 billion in 2014, when he was twenty-two years old. Luckey was certainly aware that if he built something great it would have commercial value, but he built the first version of the headset at age seventeen because he found that a good one didn't exist, and he enjoyed the challenge of making it himself.

Each of these six examples of highly creative and productive times and places was unique in its focus and consequences. One could also point to other highly fruitful eras in different parts of the world. During the early Middle Ages, for example, the Islamic world was a great center of science and mathematics, with much progress being made on the edges of the empire. But these six cases give us a basis to consider what hubs of creativity or golden ages might have in common. The next question is: Do they occur by chance, or can they be initiated and cultivated by an act of human will?

The first common feature of historical golden ages is that they have been driven by fairly small numbers of people. This idea might conflict with the egalitarian spirit of the postmodern world, but it remains true. Consequential innovations come from a relatively few people, often in small groups linked by common interests and joined in a shared purpose.

A high level of social trust enables creative people to cooperate and compete, to encourage and inspire each other.

Second, while each of the golden ages I've identified was characterized by a distinct Weltanschauung, all were marked by a resistance to stifling conformity. Curiosity and intellectual courage were highly valued by those who drove innovation. Instead of demanding adherence to consensus views, they encouraged and honored subversive energy. And there was a strong sense of *asabiyya*.

The third principle is that human agency matters. Things can change when one person sets out to make life better or push the boundaries of possibility, rather than simply accept fate or the status quo. It is true that fortune or providence enters in, but the importance of agency cannot be understated. It is also true that no one really acts alone or in a void. Michelangelo or James Watt could not have done the work for which he is known and from which others benefit without a farmer to feed him or a tailor to make his clothes, but that doesn't disprove the central proposition.

Francis Fukuyama underscored the civilizational value of those few who strive to see farther, reach higher, do better:

> A civilization devoid of anyone who wanted to be recognized as better than others, and which did not affirm in some way the essential health and goodness of such a desire, would have little art or literature, music or intellectual life. It would be incompetently governed, for few people of quality would choose a life of public service. It would not have much in the way of economic dynamism; its crafts and industries would be pedestrian and unchanging, and its technology second-rate.[6]

The question for us is how to encourage the fruitful use of the desire for distinction, and how to nurture unique talents for invention. Part of the answer lies in the educational system.

As the University of Edinburgh played a central role in the Scottish Enlightenment, Stanford University has helped advance tech innovation in Silicon Valley. Stanford, in fact, is one of several institutions founded in the late nineteenth century as a consequence of one man's recognition of a need for a new kind of educational institution to promote American progress and competitiveness.

In the late 1850s, William Barton Rogers thought the existing institutions of higher education were not meeting the needs of a growing, industrializing country. America's earliest and most prestigious universities were built on the model of Oxford and Cambridge, which had been founded as divinity schools and evolved into universities with an emphasis on the humanities or liberal arts. Harvard, Yale, and Princeton all began with the purpose of training men for Christian ministry. Even after they ceased educating ministers, the system of teaching humanities retained something like the sensibility of a seminary, albeit a secular one.

Rogers believed that America should have institutions of higher learning more focused on promoting national strength in "trade, manufactures, and the other productive arts" based on what he called "the admitted result of the superior intelligence which has inspired our enterprise and guided our activity."[7] He was inspired by the success of the German university system in producing scientific advances, and he believed that if America was to maintain and increase its material prosperity and the peace and security upon which it rested, a more intentional effort was required. He saw a need for new institutions with a specific mandate, so he founded the Massachusetts Institute of Technology in 1861. Several more universities on the same model, both public and private, followed quickly. Between 1861 and 1900, eight of the world's top universities were founded in the United States. After MIT came the first University of California campus at Berkeley (1868), Johns Hopkins University (1876), the University of California at Los Angeles (1882), the University of Chicago (1890), Stanford

University (1891), the California Institute of Technology (1891), and Carnegie Mellon University (1900).

Seven of these institutions are among the top fifteen in the *Times Higher Education* World University Rankings for 2021, while the other one (Carnegie Mellon) comes in at number twenty-eight. Over the years, their faculty, alumni, and staff have won hundreds of Nobel Prizes, Fields Medals, and Turing Awards. Stanford alone accounts for eighty-three Nobel Prizes. The public Cal Berkeley counts more Turing Awards than any Ivy League university. These institutions were crucial in educating the people who developed the technologies that propelled America forward in the great period of growth from 1870 to 1970, and in laying the groundwork for the computer revolution that has been the source of most innovation and productivity growth over the past several decades.

This same sense of mission is also present in primary and secondary education, which took on the role of teaching civil religion to create good citizens. But when the consensus over what constitutes a good citizen began to break down in the early twentieth century, the result was a multigenerational battle over curriculum. It's also why American education is broken. This mission of teaching has deemphasized things like math, hard sciences, geography, and reading, in favor of politico-religious teaching on the seminary model. If more emphasis were placed on objective subjects—which require a firm understanding of the physical world—students would finish school sooner, it would cost less, and they would find themselves better equipped for productive lives.

Rogers and others saw a need for more technical expertise and developed institutions to fill it, bringing long-term benefit to the whole society. But like their predecessors, those universities too have ossified, becoming more self-referential, cautious, and defensive. They no longer carry forward their original mission with the same focus, zeal, or effectiveness. They were purpose-built for the problems of another era, and now it's time for a refresh.

The physicist Freeman Dyson famously said that doing good science means being subversive. He's right, and it's true for every field that requires creativity. We shouldn't forget that the great artists who pursued beauty left a towering legacy: Brunelleschi or Palladio in architecture, Leonardo in painting, Michelangelo in sculpture—all had to break out of the cage to do so. It's the independent thinkers, the unusual minds—and often temperamental personalities—who drive things forward.

Faculty tenure was designed to give eccentric, even disagreeable, but brilliant people the freedom to pursue heterodox ideas and unpopular projects without fear of losing their jobs. But the university has become the bureaucratic iron cage described by Max Weber. Scholars and scientists find themselves restricted by the procedural, professional, and social constraints placed upon them by the bureaucracies that run the universities and the grant-making institutions that control the funding necessary to pursue research. Going against the grain is not appreciated. Galileo need not apply. One doesn't have to look far for examples of universities using their power to silence professors with unapproved views: Bret Weinstein was forced out of Evergreen State College when he taught a class on a day that some students had demanded white people be barred from campus. Scott Atlas, a professor at Stanford University Medical Center and a senior fellow at the Hoover Institution, was the subject of relentless attacks from colleagues and retaliation from administrators when his professional opinion on Covid—later proved right—differed from those of prominent media and political figures. The list goes on. And it is, of course, impossible to measure the extent of self-censorship this engenders among academics who see what happens to dissenters.

Men like William Barton Rogers created institutional spaces to foster Promethean creativity. But the spirit of creativity that birthed the industrial age eventually succumbed to the stifling spirit of its own invention, the assembly line. Incrementalism replaced Prometheus. The universities are now in their old age, and it's time to develop new institutions that better promote dynamism today.

Another dysfunctional aspect of modern higher education is how it has spawned "credentialism," the overreliance on an academic degree rather than more direct evidence of competence in a specific activity. Credentialism is a way of outsourcing evaluation and shifting responsibility: "How was I supposed to know he couldn't do the job? He graduated from Harvard!" As more employers came to rely on academic credentials in hiring, more people needed those credentials, the institutions that provide them grew more powerful, and the cost escalated.

A study by a market analysis firm showed a large number of employers requiring bachelor's degrees for jobs in which the degree is unnecessary for the work: "In a five-year period, jobs such as dental lab technicians and medical equipment operators saw their college degree requirements in job postings increase, in some cases by almost 175%."[8] But the incentives to keep the game going are strong, and a great many young people who don't need college for the work they choose are pulled into it nevertheless. As bachelor's degrees have become commonplace, the most ambitious may try to set themselves apart with an advanced degree. We have a surfeit of credentials and a deficit of creativity.

A college degree has become overvalued and overpriced. We're in the midst of a bubble in higher education, similar to what we saw in the housing bubble. The prevailing opinion before the crash of 2008 was that more Americans entering the housing market as buyers would lead to higher home values as well as the stability and other benefits of an "ownership society," to use President Bush's term. But this ostensibly pro-social policy led to a bubble that burst disastrously, and many people lost their homes. The higher education bubble too will either burst or deflate under the weight of its own contradictions—the product isn't worth what it costs.

The dynamics just described might be viewed in terms of a "network effect," which in the basic definition means that the value of a product increases as more people join the "network" of users. A network effect is generally understood as beneficial to an individual and often to the wider society as well. But in some cases, too many people in the network can dilute the value and introduce negative effects that overwhelm the positive ones.

The classic example of a network effect is the telephone. When few people owned a phone, the benefit was limited, but the usefulness grew as more people had one. Individuals purchased a telephone for their own benefit, but in doing so they added value to other people's phones. The internet grew on the same principle: the multiplication of participants increased its value to each user. Social media companies like Facebook, Twitter, and Snapchat have grown extremely wealthy in part because the network effect also puts up a barrier to competition when the network is proprietary (owned by the social media company). This economic effect has overshadowed the potential and real antisocial consequences of crowded networks controlled by sociopathic institutions.

Social media today are nothing more than dopamine rat mazes designed to monopolize the users' time by preying on their vanity, insecurity, and need for social validation. According to a report based on leaked documents, "Facebook showed advertisers how it has the capacity to identify when teenagers feel 'insecure', 'worthless' and 'need a confidence boost'."[9] A study by researchers at Johns Hopkins demonstrated that "the more you use Facebook, the worse you feel."[10] This is true for other social media platforms too, of course. There is also the polarizing effect that social media have had on our national politics by creating contrary hyperrealities. It's an open secret that professional journalists today spend too much time in Twitter echo chambers, and that many stories published in traditional media originated there.

Many positive network effects seem to have a limit. As the network gets too big, there's an inflection point where negative effects begin to dominate, undermining the efficacy and perhaps the viability of the network. Instead of encouraging creative production, the network begins to seek stability and conformity. That's when a network becomes weaponized and violent.

Network effects can be either beneficial or antisocial. Cultural renewal will come from creating networks with pro-social effects, to replace the sociopathic networks that currently exercise cultural hegemony, such as the universities and media companies as they currently exist. The starting point for renewal must be small, self-sustaining, perhaps even self-contained organizations that can serve as nodes of emergent networks, providing the structure, example, and perhaps the foundation of a more vital culture.

We might also think in terms of seedbeds that can blossom into something bigger. But for now, small is beautiful. Perhaps it always has been. Monasteries are small, as are even the largest monastic orders. Universities are too. The Select Society and the Poker Club in Edinburgh were small but consequential. Jesus had just twelve apostles.

Whatever form these seedbeds of renewal take, they must be characterized by *asabiyya*—a combination of solidarity, cohesion, trust, and shared purpose. The vigorous pursuit of a common goal generates a sense of joy. Veterans often remark that they miss the camaraderie of military life, with a common goal, common trials, victories and defeats in which everyone shares. But everyone has a distinct role. Everyone knows the overall mission and the part they are expected to play. The very fact of having friends who are relying on you—of having a duty to them—encourages everyone to do their best.

As the proverb says, "A friend loves at all times and a brother is born for adversity." This runs counter to the social sadism of the liberal order, but it is the basis of every vital human institution. Friends and brothers do not base their relationships primarily on what they get out of them; they are not transactional. A relationship with a friend and a brother is more durable and more satisfying for being based on grace and loyalty rather than personal benefit, utility, or happiness.

What follows is a short list of both existing and notional structures with the characteristics most likely to generate vitality. These potential seedbeds of renewal will need room to act with great independence, to develop and blossom and then reproduce. To the extent there is a role for government, it is to encourage their formation while allowing a high degree of autonomy.

There should be space for a variety of intentional communities formed around intellectual, cultural, or commercial endeavors. A few people simply starting a discussion group can be influential. Consider the Junto Club in colonial America, founded by Benjamin Franklin along with eleven friends—tradesmen and artisans—to discuss philosophical and political questions. Some years later, in 1743, Franklin gathered a group of learned men to form the American Philosophical Society, which still exists today. Early members included John Adams, Thomas Jefferson, George Washington, Alexander Hamilton, James Madison, and other luminaries. What would a twenty-first-century Junto Club look like? What would be its purpose?

Today, universities are the prime example of self-contained intellectual communities. There are other kinds in existence too, such as the scientific communities that have grown up in Los Alamos, New Mexico, and Huntsville, Alabama. The difference, perhaps, between these communities and universities is that their members share a common project and are focused on a practical outcome, which is more in keeping with the ethos that led William Barton Rogers to found MIT. It's also time to think about alternatives to the research university that are more dynamic and more effective in generating innovation. Such communities could regain the idea of science as the pursuit of wonder.

Groups formed around artistic interests can also be sources of innovation. The Pre-Raphaelite Brotherhood, formed in 1848 and encouraged by John Ruskin, had a great influence on aesthetic sensibilities. William Morris later associated himself with the Pre-Raphaelites and initiated the Arts and Crafts movement; some of his wallpaper designs are still widely used. Morris shared the utopian socialist ideas of Ruskin, which helped shape the Progressive Era on both sides of the Atlantic. I do not recommend his politics, but the influence of art on society is underappreciated.

Also in 1848, the Oneida Community was founded in New York as a utopian religious commune, initially with eighty-seven members. They practiced various crafts to support themselves, most notably making silverware, which is still manufactured today under the Oneida label long after the commune dissolved in 1881 and some members reorganized as a joint stock company. In the twentieth century, Frank Lloyd Wright influenced generations of architects first at his Ohio estate, called Taliesin, and then also at Taliesin West, built in 1937 on the outskirts of Scottsdale, Arizona. One of his students, Paolo Soleri, went on to create Arcosanti, an "urban laboratory" or experimental town in the Arizona desert designed with environmental sustainability in mind.

All these are examples of small groups led by a visionary leader, putting into practice their ideas for a better way of living, and eventually having a significant effect on the wider world. As always, it is small groups of dedicated people that change history.

Similar pioneering communities could be facilitated through the concept of charter cities, given wide latitude for experimentation in governance and economic policy. The Charter Cities Institute, inspired by the success of Singapore, Hong Kong, Shenzhen, and Dubai in developing "from impoverished to world-class cities in two to three generations," aims to encourage more urban success stories. As the institute explains, "A charter city is a city granted a special jurisdiction to create a new governance system. The purpose of the special jurisdiction is simple but powerful; it allows city officials to adopt the best practices in commercial regulation" as well as in education, transportation, health care, etc.[11] The scope should be larger: charter cities should be allowed to experiment with all aspects of governance. No charter city has been established yet, but a government that is serious about building a better future would authorize several small charter cities to form and experiment with possibilities for governance. It's also possible that some existing cities could take on a more independent status. What could New York City or Milwaukee become if they had more freedom of action?

Some seedbeds of renewal may be explicitly religious in character, or simply composed of people with similar religious commitments who cooperate enjoyably and productively. Orthodox Jews in America are an example of a community formed around religious faith. Mormons in Utah are another. Physical communities united by religion may take different forms, but they should be encouraged.

These ideas all represent in some way the intentional re-creation of a frontier, be it intellectual, commercial, religious, or artistic. The risk that comes with being on a frontier—even if it is metaphorical and there is no threatening enemy nearby—fosters a creative response to challenges. If frontier outposts of various kinds can be multiplied, their dynamism will radiate out through the larger culture.

But the first seedbed of renewal must be the family—the most essential of human organizations, the first building block of society, the most fundamental sensemaking institution, the primary transmitter of culture, and literally the source of the next generation. In ancient Greece and Rome, in early modern England, in colonial America, independent families sustaining themselves as farmers, artisans, or small-scale merchants formed a middle class that was the basis of social stability. Interrelated, extended families are the ultimate network, amplifying the benefits of family throughout the society. Strong, self-sustaining families create healthy cultures. Those qualities should be nurtured rather than demonized. Families are under constant attack in media, as these headlines illustrate: "Is Having A Baby In 2021 Pure Environmental Vandalism?" (*Vogue*).[12] "Science proves kids are bad for Earth. Morality suggests we stop having them" (NBC News).[13]

It is a shopworn truth that families have been under pressure in

America for decades. Family formation is down, fertility is down, the sense of continuity is deteriorating as more people move away from family to pursue a career. The institution of family is durable, but it needs both encouragement and autonomy. I will suggest measures to strengthen families in the final chapter.

Religion promotes family formation and stability, as the economist Tyler Cowen acknowledged in a discussion with Matthew Yglesias. Though not personally religious, Cowen said, "I think people, on average, should become more religious, in part because that would encourage fertility." Yglesias replied, "I think probably we say that religiousness is almost constitutive of right-wingy-ness, at least in some definitions. Yeah, I think a more traditionalist America, in some ways, would be good."[14] Both Cowen and Yglesias see the social benefits of religion and the robust family life that almost always accompanies it.

Religion is an indispensable element of a vital culture. In some quarters that may be controversial, even anathema, but it shouldn't be. Religion helps channel *thymos*, the drive to rise above the common lot and achieve distinction, into beneficial activity. It provides a common moral code and a shared sense of ultimate values and purpose. History shows that successful societies are unified by religion. This does not mean that minority religions are prohibited or persecuted, but it does mean that there is a clearly dominant religion that defines the culture.

It isn't hard to find examples of religious solidarity providing part of the context for generative periods in history. Most of the great projects of antiquity were religious buildings, such as the pyramids of Egypt and the Anu Ziggurat of the Uruk civilization, built around 4000 BC. In the classical era, the gods of Olympus were honored across the Hellenic world, and displays of public piety were a central aspect of the culture. In the Middle Ages, Islam was the uniting, normative feature of the society that spread from Persia to Spain and produced a flowering of science and philosophy. In Renaissance Italy, the Roman Catholic Church was a part of everyone's life, and even the religious minorities (primarily Jews and Muslims) were influenced by the Catholic culture.

Scotland during its Enlightenment had recently worked its way through serious religious and dynastic conflict, but in that furnace a fairly cohesive nation had been formed for the first time in the tumultuous history of the Scots. Caledonia had long been divided among hostile clans, but by the mid-eighteenth century there was a Scottish nation with a uniquely Scottish church. The Church of Scotland, founded by John Knox, was the common heritage of the brightest lights in the Enlightenment firmament. Though many of them, like David Hume, were at best skeptics if not outright atheists, they nonetheless shared the culture of which the Scottish church was a part. And the history of that church, which emerged in defiance of Rome, Canterbury, and the English monarch, perhaps imbued the Scots with a respect for subversive thinking.

Religion provides unity and purpose for the faithful in the pursuit of transcendent power outside of one's self. In America, Christianity broadly speaking was long the dominant religion by far. That is no longer the case. Western liberalism says that it has privatized religion, but as a practical matter, liberalism creates conditions that are hostile to religion. In the name of tolerance and an end to violence based, it asserts, on religious differences, liberalism has coerced people into either abandoning religion or subordinating it to the demands of liberalism itself. This has had the effect of atomizing society and corrosive effect on the individual.

When stripped of something bigger than themselves, something that they have a duty to serve, people become self-referential. Thus we have the postmodern culture of narcissism in a consumer society. This is not sustainable. Narcissists don't plant trees under which they will never sit. Why would they? They are far less likely to marry, less likely to stay married if they do marry, and they have fewer children. But they do order lots of takeout meals for one, pay their monthly subscriptions to Netflix, and are available to work late because there's no one at home waiting for them. Only 28 percent of Americans ages 18–34 years are married, compared with 59 percent in 1978, according to census data, and the baby bust, characterized by subreplacement fertility rates, has been ongoing for many years.[15] Man either looks up or he looks in. And the interiority of postmodern life is one of its most troubling, most corrosive features.

Late-stage liberalism imitates religion by seeking enemies to defeat and scapegoats to be sacrificed for the atonement of the many. The result is a steady stream of moral panics that culminate in a kind of ritual sacrifice of a designated sinner. But the ritual cycle fractures rather than unites civil society. In foreign policy, the syndrome manifests in a sort of moral imperialism that increases friction with competitor societies.

The secularism that is one of the hallmarks of the liberal world is an anomalous fork in the path of human history; it has no precedent. It is insistently defined as a form of "progress," but toward what? Freedom is one of the answers. Or justice. While both of those are real concepts, in this context they are just slogans meant to mystify the discourse. Rather, the zealous insistence that secularism is "progress," understood as "better than yesterday but not as good as tomorrow," belies the brittleness of the secular world.

The vectors of decay are powerful and have been visible for a long time on many fronts: in chronic disease, poor educational outcomes despite much higher per-capita spending than peer nations, real wages that have grown only very slowly for decades and even then most of the growth has been for higher earners while lower earners have dropped further behind, dying cities and towns across the American interior, wealth concentration accelerating to levels that have been historically correlated with political dysfunction and breakdown, ineffective, self-serving institutions, parasitic elites, low social trust, anemic family formation, low fertility rates, and a rising concentration of political, cultural, and economic power in a largely insulated ruling caste. But America started out with deep reserves of social trust, political stability, and material wealth—and the country still has a large number of energetic and talented people of good will. So despite all of the things heading in the wrong direction, there are also some things that have been going in a positive direction. There are bright spots to note and promising developments to encourage. We can build upon them with bigger, bolder ideas for moving forward.

BIG COUNTRY, BIG PROJECTS

MARC ANDREESSEN, THE VENTURE CAPITALIST, WROTE A blogpost in early 2020 titled "It's Time to Build." It drew much comment, mostly favorable. Even the critics agreed with Andreessen's sentiment but were skeptical that America still has the capacity to build. Still, the piece struck a chord and raised expectations for what might be possible if we set big goals and dare to act. The question is what to build: New software? New hardware? AI? Self-driving cars? Strong churches? Strong families? Art? Architecture? Strong towns? New and better towns? All of them?

There are two choices: better or worse, development or decay. There is no neutral. So, Andreessen is right. If we don't like things the way they are—and surveys consistently show that supermajorities of Americans think the country is on the wrong track—then we need to build something better.

People with a bold vision and the drive to realize it are inspirational. Many find Elon Musk charismatic because he has big ideas, states them clearly, and then sets about achieving them. Musk founded a solar energy company (Solar City), an electric car company (Tesla), a space exploration company (SpaceX), and a company to build loop intercity transportation systems (The Boring Company). These companies are building game-changing technologies. For example, SpaceX's Falcon 9 rocket was a huge improvement over every competitor when it was first launched in 2010. And its successor, the Falcon Heavy, is even better. It can deliver payloads to low-earth orbit for around $1,400 per kilogram, about one-third the cost of its nearest competitor and far less than the $54,000 per kilogram cost for NASA's Space Shuttle. The company's new Starship rocket is even more efficient and will lower the cost to around $10 per kilogram, which permits a lot of applications that were previously cost-prohibitive. SpaceX's Starlink, which will provide inexpensive satellite internet service worldwide, would have been impossible without these low-cost launches. Combine that rocket technology with the tunneling technology being developed by the Boring Company and you have the possibility of mining mineral-rich meteors and the beginnings of the tools for colonizing Mars, which is one of Musk's goals. He also has had seven children. He is creative in every sense.

Big projects create their own gravitational field and draw people to them, but we need more visionary, charismatic, energetic leadership to propel such projects. We have been training managers rather than builders for a long time, and it has led to a culture of risk aversion, of asking "How do I cover my ass?" rather than "How do we get this done?" That must change. We need an educational system and an incentive structure that better cultivates builders and creators.

Financialization has badly misallocated resources and left America poorer for it. Among other things it has led many of America's smartest and most ambitious people to put their considerable talents into creating complex mechanisms for extracting money from the productive economy, rather than creating new products that generate wealth by improving lives. There is a significant difference between inventing penicillin or the automobile and creating a financial derivative for speculating on the mortgages taken out by people with shabby credit histories. In a financialized economy, the focus is on money. But as Elon Musk put it succinctly, "The thing we call money is just an information system for labor allocation. What actually matters is making goods & providing services."[1] We have also allowed a virtual world to dominate much of our lives. A decade ago, Marc Andreessen wrote that software was "eating the world," and it's even more true today. The world of bits has encouraged a radical, neognostic, self-referential and destructive interiority. We need to reengage our natural sociability and focus on projects that improve our physical lives and the natural world around us.

It's hard to look back at the past several decades and not conclude that the purported progress in difficult-to-measure areas like justice, equality, equity, respect, and self-esteem has been a distraction from the lack of improvement or even decay in easy-to-measure, real-world things like physical health, longevity, family formation, fertility rates, real income, home ownership, debt levels, and so forth. In this chapter I want to look at some projects and ideas that are large and ambitious but focused on bringing material improvements in American life.[2]

Powering the Future

Cheap, abundant energy has historically improved living standards and served as a catalyst for innovation. Steam power was key to propelling the first Industrial Revolution. In the twentieth century, electrification gave a massive boost to productivity and prosperity. Without it, there would be no computers or any of the enhanced productivity (or distractions) they have enabled. Even a brief power outage makes us aware of how much our daily routines depend on electricity.

About 60 percent of the electric power now used in the United States comes from burning hydrocarbons (fossil fuel), mostly coal and natural gas. Petroleum, another hydrocarbon, fuels the internal combustion engine, powering most of the transportation sector and roughly a quarter of the industrial sector. Hydrocarbons provided power many orders of magnitude greater than anything previously available, changing human society to a degree that is impossible to overstate. Fossil fuel dramatically reduced the amount of labor that goes into producing a bushel of wheat. It changed the way cities are built and how war is waged. But we've reached the limits of what's possible with hydrocarbon-based energy. The price can't really go significantly lower for any sustained period of time. Coal is still abundant in the United States, but it comes with downsides for health and the environment. Developing a new source of energy that is cheap, abundant, and sustainable should be a top priority. A power source that's an order of magnitude cheaper and more abundant than hydrocarbons would propel a new age of abundance.

The good news is that there has been a lot of progress in alternative energy in the past few years. Technologies for harnessing wind and solar power are improving: the newest utility-scale wind and solar installations using the most advanced commercially available technology have production costs for electricity below 4 cents per kilowatt hour. That's less than half the cost of electricity from coal and conventional nuclear power. But wind and solar power both have well-known shortcomings and limitations. Wind turbines kill great numbers of birds, they require a lot of land, they're ugly, and they cause noise pollution. The turbines must be built in locations with a lot of wind, which will be inconsistent in any case. During the winter storm that hit the South and the Midwest in February 2021, the wind turbines in Texas froze while demand for electricity spiked in the unusually low temperatures. As for solar power, it is practical only where there is plenty of sunshine, and even there the solar panels produce little electricity when it's cloudy and none at night.

Solar and wind can both be part of the nation's energy plan, but they can't produce anywhere near enough baseload power for the whole country even at current levels of demand. That's one of the reasons that some people have focused so much attention on reducing energy use. In a nation where all the cars are electric, which many hope to see, the amount of electricity produced with hydrocarbons today would not suffice—much less would solar and wind power. If we want to run electric cars for the whole country and much else besides on clean energy, we will need a new source that is low-cost, plentiful, and steady around the clock.

Hydropower is cheap and clean, but only a limited number of places can produce it. A safe nuclear fusion reactor has been a dream of many for decades, though little effort is being put into fusion research. A small-scale fusion reactor is set to come on line in 2030, and in the best-case scenario it would take decades after that for this technology to make a difference. There is also promising new fission technology in so-called mini-reactors. Should we pursue nuclear? Without a doubt. We should also pursue promising technologies in geothermal energy: tapping the heat energy stored in the earth's crust. It's clean and essentially unlimited. With the technology now being developed, it may be far cheaper than any other major energy source. Geothermal power might lead the next energy revolution.

If it does, everything else will change. Companies that are developing the means to capture geothermal energy, such as Sage Geosystems, say that the initial cost per kilowatt hour will be around 3.5 cents. That's comparable with the cost of solar and wind in the newest installations, but much lower than the roughly 9.5 cents per kilowatt hour for coal and nuclear power from existing plants. Geothermal is baseload energy, available at all times regardless of weather or time of day, and geothermal plants could be built almost anywhere. What's more, the cost of geothermal energy from existing installations may drop after the initial capital is returned because the "wells" never run dry and don't have to be re-dug. The prospect of ultracheap, superabundant, always-on geothermal power is a game-changer. Transportation and manufacturing costs would drop dramatically and make the broad adoption of electric cars feasible too.

Advances in battery technology will also facilitate a transition to electric vehicles. A new kind of lithium-ion battery that doesn't use cobalt, which is rare and expensive, could replace those currently in use. That would lower the price of electric cars, increase their range to 500 miles or more on a single charge, reduce charging time to ten minutes, and extend the life of the battery to as much as a million miles. Electric cars would then outperform gas-powered ones on every metric: lower purchase price, lower operating and maintenance costs, better performance, and longer life. Electric cars have much faster acceleration, and the 2021 Tesla Model-S Plaid is set to achieve a top speed near 200 miles per hour.

Auto manufacturers are moving away from conventional powertrains toward electric, partly because of concern about emissions but mostly because new technology is making electric vehicles better all around. Jaguar has announced that all of its new cars will be electric by 2025, and 60 percent of Land Rovers will be electric by 2030.

Going forward, new technologies will be preferred simply because they're better. Even the world's major oil and gas companies have already recast themselves as "energy" companies. In September 2020, BP issued a report saying that global oil demand may have peaked the previous year and predicting a long-term secular decline, after a temporary post-Covid uptick, even as overall demand for power increases.

It's time to rebuild America's energy infrastructure. We should undertake an initiative to double electricity production by 2050 and build a nationwide smart electric grid. We might call the project Edison 2050. At least 60 percent of the new capacity should come from geothermal plants. A new national grid has an estimated cost of $5 trillion (less than the U.S. government allocated for Covid-related spending), and it's safe to assume that building the facilities to double the nation's electricity production would cost as much. But the payoff would be enormous after a few years. The total cost of electricity at current levels of use would drop by nearly $1 trillion per year, but meanwhile demand will increase, especially if electric cars become the norm. This means that the investment would pay for itself in well under a decade and then bring straightforward savings.

There are also more unpredictable but likely benefits, since new sources of cheap power have always spurred broader innovation in the past. This time should be no different, and America should lead the way.

Life and Health—America100

What greater goal could we have than longer and healthier life for Americans?

America100 should be made of three parts: life extension therapy that focuses on rejuvenation as well as the prevention and cure of chronic disease. In the past few generations, chronic diseases have reached epidemic proportions in the United States—especially diseases associated with chronic inflammation, such as diabetes, arthritis, cardiovascular disease, autoimmune disorders, and some cancers. Six in ten American adults now have a chronic disease—a 700 percent increase since 1935. And 40 percent of American adults have two or more chronic diseases.[3] These diseases are far less common in other countries.

Much work has been done on treating these diseases, but more attention should be paid to avoiding them in the first place. A big part of the blame can be placed on American lifestyles, especially the sedentary, mostly indoor lives that have become the norm. Worse still is the typical American diet, filled with factory foods that promote inflammation and diseases, especially foods high in simple carbohydrates and processed sugars such as corn syrup, which raise blood sugar levels and promote insulin resistance. The rapid increase in chronic disease has also coincided with a 150-fold increase in consumption of vegetable oils.[4] Of particular concern are seed oils such as rapeseed oil (canola), cottonseed oil (once used as an industrial solvent), sunflower oil, and palm oil, in place of natural fats like butter and lard as well as olive oil and coconut oil.

Unfortunately, the current medical system incentivizes treatment more than prevention. Pharmaceutical companies are only too happy to sell drugs for preventable diseases that were virtually unknown in earlier times. You've seen the television commercials for some new drug to "manage" a diet-related chronic disease. There's a vague promise of improvement, followed by a list of horrible side effects:

Global Consumption of Vegetable Oil, 1909–2019

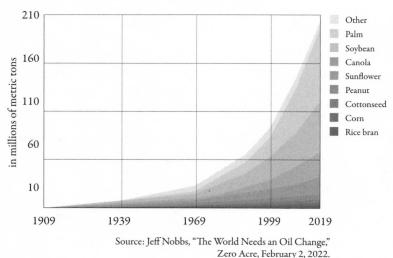

Source: Jeff Nobbs, "The World Needs an Oil Change,"
Zero Acre, February 2, 2022.

Cheerful Announcer: "Take Positiviron for the management of daily unwellness."

Speed-Talking Voiceover: "Side effects may include hair loss, numbness, tingling, extreme fatigue, restlessness, hot flashes, cold spells, fever, blurred vision, sleeplessness, nausea, cramping, sunburn, ringing in the ears, deafness, loss of sexual function, suicidal thoughts, stuffy nose, welts, warts, corns, and itchiness."

Does that sound like a prescription for a long, vital life?

It doesn't have to be this way, but the solution is not simply a new food pyramid or a revised set of dietary guidelines. Industrial agriculture is making Americans fatter and sicker, leading to premature death. People like John Durant, the Harvard-educated evolutionary psychologist and author of *The Paleo Manifesto*, are rediscovering ancient wisdom about how to optimize the function of the human body, and adding a deeper understanding of biology to what was previously known by intuition and practiced by tradition. Ray Peat was one of the modern pioneers of such research. Justin and Erica Sonnenburg, professors at Stanford and authors of *The Good Gut*, have done groundbreaking research that shows how we can live longer and healthier lives by enhancing the function of our bodies' natural systems.

At the same time, significant advances are being made in biomedical science, and the pace of discovery may be accelerating. Over the next two decades we might see life-improving innovation at the same rate as what happened in the world of bits over the last twenty years. And it won't be about taking more drugs. Currently, however, the institutions that regulate the use of biomedical advances lack the capacity to keep up. Encouraging more and faster progress in this area would serve America well.

Gene editing is a new approach to curing disease that has particularly exciting potential with the recent discovery of the CRISPR-Cas9 system. CRISPR stands for "clusters of regularly interspaced short palindromic repeats," a specialized stretch of DNA. The CRISPR technology is adapted from a naturally occurring defense mechanism in bacteria, and it makes gene editing more accurate and efficient than earlier methods.[5] Once it was understood that cancer is caused by changes in DNA, researchers began investigating therapies using CRISPR gene editing. The National Cancer Institute reported: "The first trial in the United States to test a CRISPR-made cancer therapy was launched in 2019 at the University of Pennsylvania. The study, funded in part by NCI, is testing a type of immunotherapy in which patients' own immune cells are genetically modified to better 'see' and kill their cancer."[6] There are promising CRISPR therapies for other disorders including sickle-cell anemia and thalassemia, and a potential for reversing blindness caused by retinal degeneration. CRISPR has risks and unknowns, but those are being identified, quantified, and minimized.

One of the most exciting areas of research right now is life extension. Not long ago the idea was considered crackpot, but recent breakthroughs make it more than plausible. New therapies are already making some difference at the margin, and more appears to be within reach in the next few years.

One study has found that it's possible to rejuvenate the thymus with human growth hormone. The thymus is critical to the immune system, and its decay is a key part of the aging process. The study "found that 12 months of treatment created about 2.5 years of epigenetic rejuvenation, with results accelerating in the last quarter of the trial."[7] Therapeutic plasma exchange—removing plasma and replacing it with saline and albumin—has also shown a capacity to "rejuvenate germ layer tissues and improve cognition by reducing neuroinflammation."[8] There are so many other promising possibilities under investigation that Lifespan.io publishes a "Rejuvenation Roadmap" tracking all of the research and experimental therapies in development. It's an amazingly long list. Significant resources, both public and private, should be devoted to pushing this science forward and distributing effective therapies widely.

We could undertake a comprehensive national project—let's call it America100—with the goal that average Americans can live healthy, active lives to the century mark and beyond. Pursuing this aim should be a national priority. A median life expectancy of 100 years suggests that the oldest people would live perhaps as long as 150 years. Of course, nobody wants to live that long if it means decades of cognitive decline and bodily impairment, so it's important that people remain healthy and capable of mentally and physically active lives at ages where that is generally considered impossible, or highly unusual. Everyone wants to be healthier, but some people question the value of more life than the eighty or so years we now expect.

Why live longer? A Christian would answer that with more life one can give more glory to God. This would make no sense to an atheist, but both could agree that there is something electric about life that makes us generally want to keep it rather than lose it, and that life can bring great joy. There are things we can do not just to extend it but to increase the joy of living.

Family: Haven in a Heartless World—Generation21

One thing that brings great joy and makes us love life is other people, and particularly family. It is the most basic unit of human life, and it is within the family—our haven in a heartless world—that we fulfill many of our most essential and most rewarding roles: husband, wife, father, mother, son, daughter, brother, sister. Reinvigorating the family is a way of revitalizing America.

Every family is a society in miniature. It is a decentralized locus of authority and discipline, unity and stability. Families are the basic building block of the larger society. They also produce positive network effects, starting within the nuclear family, then the extended family, and then further outward. A society plagued by family breakdown and lower family formation sees lower network effects and more sociopathology, less overall social cohesion, and a lower capacity for collective action. Loneliness and atomization don't just carry personal costs; they are a vector of social decay. The best way—perhaps the only way—to reverse this is to reinvigorate the family by making it easier for families to form and to thrive. A project for doing so might be called Generation21.

One of the main obstacles to family formation—though by no means the only one—is economic. Generation21 should have some simple goals: rebuild the country and its economy so that a single median wage is sufficient to support a family of four, own a home and a car, pay for health care and college tuition, and buy the other essentials of life. Oren Kass called this the cost of thriving. Since the mid-1980s it has grown harder to thrive in America. We should also strive for a total fertility rate of 2.25, a bit above the replacement rate. The last time we achieved that rate was 1971. If we're able to fix the economic element, that may be possible.

How can we do that? The first step is to name the goal. For too long, America has tied success to increasing the number of adults in the workforce and keeping wages low, in response to the consequences of globalization and secular stagnation. That must reverse. One step is to recognize that kin-work in the home is essential to national vitality and social solidarity. The social messaging of the past fifty years has said that wage work outside the home is more valuable, more important, more rewarding, and more dignified than kin-work inside the home. That's false and destructive.

Recognizing the value of caretaking work in the home is a necessary predicate to reordering the political economy toward a family wage. We had it once. We can have it again.

In the meantime, there are provisional and prudential measures that can be taken to promote family formation. Economic support to make it easier to raise children has been tried across Europe and in other countries that have low fertility rates. The support has included a cash allowance paid by government to parents for each child up to the age of eighteen, down payment assistance to buy a family home, and even lifetime exemption from income tax for women who have a certain number of children. These programs have had some success at the margin and could serve as a bridge to a time when the economy is reoriented toward a family wage. For that to happen, we need to value children and the nonwage labor of their parents enough to make it a priority. We must decide to be a nation of families rather than a nation of consumers.

To achieve this goal, America must chart an independent course that makes the nation strong, self-sustaining, and resilient. Subsidies like those described above will be helpful only as part of a comprehensive program that includes ending mass immigration into the country and the export of critical manufacturing capacity abroad. If we can achieve it, we'll find that our prosperity is more durable, our society is more stable, and our lives are more fulfilling.

Teaching, Learning, Doing

Real per capita spending on primary and secondary education is higher in the United States than in nearly every peer country, yet educational outcomes have lagged for decades, often by a wide margin. K–12 education still largely reflects the spirit of the industrial age, when everything was to be homogenized and standardized for maximum efficiency of production. This was just as true for schools as it was for auto factories and steel mills. Education theorists of the early twentieth century, like Wilhelm Wundt and John Dewey, explicitly adopted the factory model with the aim of cultivating the employees and managers needed in the industrial enterprises of the day. Ellwood Cubberley, dean of the Stanford Graduate School of Education from 1917 to 1933, put it this way: "Our schools are, in a sense, factories in which the raw products (children) are to be shaped and fashioned into products to meet the various demands of life. The specifications for manufacturing come from the demands of 20th-century civilization, and it is the business of the school to build its pupils according to the specifications laid down."[9] We need a different model for a postindustrial age.

Higher education is littler better. We have some of the finest research universities in the world, but a college education typically costs too much, for too little economic return. It leaves too many young people saddled with debt they could have avoided. College also takes too long, delaying adult self-sufficiency in favor of extended adolescence. To a large degree, it functions mainly as a gatekeeper, bestowing a credential that opens doors regardless of whether the learning it represents is necessary or useful. Joseph Fuller, a professor at the Harvard Business School, found overreliance on academic credentials to be "a substantive and widespread phenomenon that is making the U.S. labor market more inefficient."[10] In the competition for credentials, increasing numbers pursue advanced degrees as a way of setting themselves apart from the merely college educated. We have a surfeit of credentials and a shortage of builders and innovators.

Many of the highest-achieving innovators skipped college or dropped out before getting a degree—Bill Gates, Michael Dell, and Mark Zuckerberg are the best known. Two Irish brothers, Patrick and John Collison, dropped out of MIT and Harvard respectively after starting a software business, and then went on to found Stripe, a web payment company. Austin Russell dropped out of Stanford and founded Luminar Technologies, which makes autonomous vehicle sensors. Vitalik Buterin, a Russian-Canadian, left college to cofound Ethereum, an open-source blockchain with smart contract functionality. Russell and Buterin both received a Thiel Fellowship, established by Peter Thiel to encourage visionaries to leave school and put their energies into their creative projects.

Recently, more young people have evidently been deciding that college is not the best way forward for them, as enrollment was declining even before the big hit from Covid-19. Change is coming. Starting in 2025 there will be fewer high school graduates who could fill incoming college classes owing to declining fertility rates. Many colleges will be more strained financially, especially the smaller ones—which in many cases are financially marginal operations already—while the largest and the most elite universities become relatively more powerful. But the demographic trend could provide an incentive for lower-tier schools to reform higher education by adopting a model that better meets the needs of students and the society today.

For starters, there must be a clear sense of mission, as there was during the last two periods of founding and reform in higher education. We must renounce credentialism. This will not be easy, since the professional and financial incentives in higher education favor producing more degrees regardless of their real value to those who earn them. So long as the students keep coming and the tuition payments keep flowing, there is no incentive to change the model. When applicant numbers shrink and the money flow dries up, there may be attentive ears to reforms suggested by outsiders, as well as space for new institutions built on a different concept.

We must be clear about what higher education should be providing in the twenty-first century, and we should also recognize that many young people would do well to skip college and acquire skills in a trade instead. The average electrician earns around $60,000 per year, starts a career earlier than a college graduate, and has no college debt. A skilled trade can also be a path to owning a small business and gaining some independence. We should be promoting practical and affordable alternatives to college, such as trade schools and apprenticeship programs.

Some visionaries have stepped up to provide educational resources that better meet the needs of students at all levels. A leader in remote learning has been the Khan Academy, a nonprofit that offers free individual lessons and full courses in subjects ranging from American history to calculus to

Elizabethan English literature—basically everything you would find in elementary and secondary school. The courses are of such high quality that teachers use them to supplement their classes in conventional schools. Students turn to Khan for extra help, such as a free tutor. Homeschooling parents use it as a resource in areas where their own knowledge is inadequate.

The Khan Academy reported large increases in use in 2020, when homeschooling and micro-schools became commonplace because of Covid, though remote learning was growing rapidly before then. While homeschooling is not for everyone, high-quality online resources make it feasible for more people. Students can learn at their own pace, spend more time on certain topics if needed, and investigate subjects that particularly interest them, in a spirit of independent discovery that is typically lacking in traditional education. Parents also gain more independence in directing their children's education.

Another online learning platform called Udemy offers subjects more likely to be found in universities and vocational schools, such as IT and software development, business and finance, video production and graphic design, along with music, art, and personal development. Udemy charges a small fee for each of its 130,000 classes, and the company, like the Khan Academy, reported substantial growth in 2020.

Khan and Udemy both offer a more bespoke, student-centered model of education that encourages independence and curiosity. A different approach comes from the Lambda School, which focuses more specifically on technical career training.

Lambda offers two main instructional tracks online: data science and full stack web development. Each can be completed in sixth months of full-time enrollment or a year part-time. In addition, a course in backend development takes nine months at full-time. Students have the opportunity to "build real products with real teams" as they learn technical skills that are in high demand and earn good wages. They have three options for paying tuition: they can pay it all upfront, or pay in installments, or defer payment with an income share agreement to pay 17 percent of their income for twenty-four months after they land a technology job paying $50,000 or more. The payments end when one of the following occurs: a) the student's payments total $30,000; b) the student has made payments of 17 percent for five years; or c) the student has not found a technology job in five years. The Lambda School turns the traditional model of higher education on its head by moving quickly, focusing on high-value skills, and putting the financial risk on the school rather than on the student.

Options like Lambda, Udemy, and the Khan Academy are not comprehensive answers to the nation's educational deficiencies, but they are part of the solution.

It's not enough simply to decry the status quo. Here are more ideas for improving education in America more broadly:

1) Streamline primary and secondary education so it culminates in year 10 (age 16) rather than year 12 (age 18).

2) Make the bachelor's degree a three-year program, and also offer the option of an express bachelor's degree that can be completed in two years of full-time school, in every field. This could be done by eliminating general education requirements. These measures would lower costs, allow students to focus on what is essential to their purposes, and let them start their productive lives sooner.

3) Establish robust career and technical training pathways both in existing institutions and in newly created ones, in partnership with business. These programs could train industrial machinery mechanics, midlevel tech workers (such as computer network architects), and workers for advanced manufacturing in life sciences, for example. Students would acquire valuable skills with a definitive career path. A national program of this kind would enable us to rebuild manufacturing capacity lost over the past few decades and would boost technological innovation.

4) Expand the use of remote learning. We've been through a nationwide experiment in online education. It can work well in many cases, particularly at the college level. It allows students to: a) take courses without relocating; b) reduce their expenses; c) time-shift classes, watching lectures

on their own schedule; d) use video conferencing to participate in discussions, seminars, and office hours.

5) Create a college equivalency exam along the lines of the GED. Many jobs are advertised as requiring a college degree, with no specifics given about the skills it is assumed to represent. The degree requirement is a filter, and its function could just as well be served by an exam and a credential similar in form to the GED. This would allow more people to apply for those jobs without the investment of time and money that college demands.

6) Require that lawful speech be unconstrained in academic settings. A university must permit vigorous debate if it is going to be a place for seeking truth.

Small Is Beautiful: Blockchain-Based Decentralization

The internet, like everything else—wealth, political power, cultural authority—has been concentrating for a long time. That's both stifling and destabilizing. Decentralized systems are generally considered both more dynamic and more durable, being more adept at overcoming challenges. They can move quickly and adapt to changing circumstances. They are more fault-tolerant and more resistant to attack, since there's no central point of control on which the whole thing hinges. In addition, they are more resistant to collusion than centralized systems.

Decentralization lowers the risk of systemic failure, increases the speed of decision making, and allows for focused local responses to emergent issues and persistent problems. That's why long-enduring imperial powers like Rome, Byzantium, and the Hapsburgs delegated substantial power to local authorities. Decentralized systems are less reliant on trust in a single source of authority. Rome was adept at incorporating new peoples and territories into the empire while leaving local social and power structures largely in place, though answerable to the emperor.

A recent and potentially transformative application of this principle is blockchain, a technology that can provide a decentralized means of performing a wide range of functions.[11] It is best known as the basis for cryptocurrencies like Bitcoin and the Ethereum network's Ether, but other applications can help create decentralized systems throughout American society.

Decentralized Finance: Any traditional financial activity—such as borrowing, lending, or trading—can be done between parties on blockchain with "smart contracts," bypassing intermediary institutions. A smart contract is a program or protocol that automatically executes or documents particular actions when conditions stipulated by the agreement are met.

Established institutions may find smart contracts useful too. For example, the global insurance company AXA experimented with a smart insurance contract that covered flight cancellation. Information on cancellations is publicly available through air traffic databases. When a covered flight was canceled, the affected policyholders were automatically paid, with no claim process, no delay, and no employee hours required. Besides being more efficient, a smart contract increases transparency and reduces error and opportunity for fraud.

Decentralized finance (DeFi) is an exit from the power of Wall Street and a way to roll back the financialization of the economy that has led to malinvestment of resources. It would reduce the rent seeking that distorts both markets and politics. In combination with decentralized currency, DeFi would neutralize the Cantillon effect by which insiders are rewarded and wealth is redistributed upward.

Decentralized Media and Internet. Centralized control of information media limits the power and reach of outsiders. The original promise of the internet and social media was to decentralize the flow of information, bypassing narrative gatekeepers. But the companies that began as platforms on which the users could create media unimpeded and unedited became new gatekeepers themselves. The internet has largely become a world of feudal domains where powerful nobility in walled castles lord it over the peasants outside. Turning it into a closed system wouldn't be too hard.

Imagine what would happen if Microsoft, Google, Apple, and Mozilla all pushed an update to their web browsers that eliminated the address bar. The open internet would effectively be closed. You might be clever and think, "I'll just use the Brave or Tor browser I've already downloaded." Sorry, but when Apple and Microsoft pushed the browser update they also made those browsers incompatible with their operating systems. You could work around the obstacle with some technical skill and Linux machines, but for all practical purposes the internet would have become the property of a few global corporations that would determine what you see. And it could all be accomplished with some simple changes and pushed out in a mandatory software update that takes effect while you're sleeping. The internet age could end without a whimper.

Media built on blockchain instead would be decentralized by the very nature of the technology. Balaji Srinivasan described how a blockchain internet could work:

> The ledger of record is the set of all cryptographically signed feeds of on-chain data. It subsumes social media feeds, data APIs, event streams, newsletters, RSS. It'll take years to build, but will ultimately become the decentralized layer of facts that underpins all narrative. Think of the ledger of record as a decentralized wire service. Every person & organization slowly moves from posting to centralized social media platforms to posting to decentralized protocols. The latter have monetization, permissions, distribution, and programmability built in.[12]

Blockchain would neuter not just the media gatekeepers but also the market-dominant companies (often actual or near monopolies) that control critical infrastructure or tools like Amazon Web Services (AWS), Cloudflare, Twilio, and so forth. A decentralized internet built on blockchain would revive the original promise of a free exchange of information.

Decentralization can provide a more robust, transparent, and stable basis for establishing facts. And it is from those facts that a more reliable narrative can be formed. Media today is powerful because it controls both

the establishment and dissemination of facts—of *what is accepted* as true—
and the forming of narrative. But the pretension of Olympian objectivi-
ty in presenting facts is something that no one believes. Decentralization
separates and clarifies the establishment of fact from meaning-making or
narrative control.

Decentralization would make the internet more secure because it
couldn't be hacked through a few or even many nodes. It would also reinvigorate the web-enabled growth and innovation that have slowed down as
the internet has become more centralized and proprietary. A new secular
cycle of value creation would be set in motion and the country would be
more prosperous, more stable, and more secure.

TomorrowLand

Every contractor will tell you that it's easier, faster, and cheaper to build
new than to remodel. If you've ever worked on fixing up an older house,
you know it's true. When you start stripping the walls, you find that there's
wallpaper over paint over plaster over who knows what. It's similar with
many older institutions, so the idea of starting afresh and building new is
tantalizing. And what about an old city with its many institutions? Maybe
there's a sound structure beneath the sluggish layers of bureaucracy and
the dust of inertia, and we could revitalize what's worth keeping. Or could
we build new cities? The creative act of building a city and its institutions
brings its own set of benefits. By definition, it requires risk-taking, energy,
innovation, and the ability to deal rapidly with unforeseen problems. A
new city, created from scratch and with a mandate for political innovation,
would be its own frontier. The opportunity to escape from owned space
and build something new would be a magnet for high achievers. It can't be
the stultifying Brasilia, but instead a Constantinople, a city built to serve
as the center of a vital civilization.

The city has been the main engine of cultural vitality at least since the
Sumerian city of Uruk dominated southern Mesopotamia (ca. 4100–2900
BC) and produced the first known written records. Cities are dynamic

places where ideas can be exchanged and where opportunities and benefits for inhabitants multiply as the population grows, in a kind of network effect. But destructive forces are amplified too, and when decline starts it can be difficult to stop. On the other hand, a city government is close to the problems it is tasked with solving. A city is small enough to move quickly in applying new ideas or changing course, yet big enough to make experiments meaningful.

Mayor Francis Suarez has aimed to turn Miami into a city that innovates and encourages innovators. One of his initiatives is to make his city the first to adopt the use of cryptocurrencies. In early 2021 he proposed three initial steps: 1) allowing city employees to be paid in crypto; 2) permitting city residents to pay their taxes and fees in crypto; 3) adding crypto assets to the city's balance sheet. Suarez has openly courted the blockchain community; he even posted Satoshi Nakamato's 2008 white paper proposing the cryptocurrency concept ("Bitcoin: A Peer-to-Peer Electronic Cash System") on the city website. His explicit goal is for Miami to become the epicenter of the blockchain world. There is an irony here, in that the ultimate promise of blockchain is to decentralize everything it touches, but Suarez wants to create a legal safe harbor that provides regulatory certainty, drawing those involved in blockchain to live in Miami. People have to be somewhere, after all, and a friendly jurisdiction in which to incubate new ideas and collaborate on projects has its advantages.

From a governance perspective, the adoption of blockchain technology in a large city could have interesting and unexpected consequences. The best outcome would be that Miami serves as a large-scale beta test of how the widespread use of blockchain—from cryptocurrency like Bitcoin to smart contracts built on Ethereum—could raise living standards, improve trust and transparency, and produce better governance outcomes. That's not guaranteed, but it's possible.

The example of Miami under an energetic young mayor is one that could be emulated in other cities. Existing institutions and commitments can supply a base of stability, but also get in the way of innovation. The "charter cities" concept mentioned earlier is one way of circumventing that problem, since the city would have "special jurisdiction to create a new governance system." If city developers build on undeveloped land, as the Charter Cities Institute explains, they "avoid the political challenges of implementing a new governance system in an existing city."[13]

Nevada has a lot of undeveloped land, making it a good place to offer enterprising people the chance to build new communities from scratch. In early 2021, Governor Steve Sisolak announced a proposal for creating "Innovation Zones" in Nevada, aiming to attract "new companies creating groundbreaking technologies" as a way of boosting the state's economy instead of relying on the familiar silver bullets like casinos or stadiums. The term may sound like the Opportunity Zones of a generation ago, but the concept is entirely different. Opportunity Zones were based on offering low tax rates to qualifying businesses that relocated within their boundaries, in the hope that those businesses would then attract further development and lead to urban revitalization. In practice, Opportunity Zones were boondoggles that benefited the people who figured out how to game the system. Nevada's Innovation Zones would not offer tax breaks, but other incentives, especially flexibility.

Sisolak notes that the existing governmental forms under state law "are inadequate alone to provide the flexibility and resources conducive to making the State a leader in attracting and retaining new forms and types of businesses and fostering economic development in emerging technologies and innovative industries."[14] Instead of seeking workarounds to sidestep structural obstacles, Innovation Zones would allow a cutting-edge company or an individual developer to build a semi-autonomous jurisdiction, within certain parameters.

First, an Innovation Zone "must be organized around the development of a particular type of technological innovation, such as the blockchain, renewable energy, and others."[15] The list also includes autonomous technology, the Internet of Things, robotics, artificial intelligence, wireless technology, biometrics, and renewable resources. It should also include biomedical science, though the state authority overseeing the program can add to the list and make ad hoc exceptions.

An Innovation Zone must begin with a minimum of 50,000 contiguous acres (78 square miles) of undeveloped land that has no permanent residents. It would be given the powers normally held by a local government and would gradually take on all the functions permitted to counties in Nevada. It must follow state and federal law, but otherwise could operate as an independent jurisdiction, doing things like building and maintaining roads, running schools, even operating police forces. The zone would have considerable latitude to innovate in all these areas of governance.

The possibility of building a new city from the ground up is tantalizing. Some of Charles Marohn's ideas for "Good Urbanism" and "Strong Towns" could be applied on a scale big enough to see what works and what doesn't. Imagine a new walkable city in a lush terraformed landscape powered by cheap, abundant geothermal electricity. That may sound like fantasy, but we need to think boldly and create spaces where visionaries can test their ideas.

The initiatives in Nevada and Miami show what might be accomplished when forward-thinking leaders have a vision and act upon it. They're not enough to reverse all the trajectories of decay, but they're a start. It's time to build new cities with wide latitude for innovation. Doing this would require the acquiescence of state and federal governments. Every state should adopt model charter language, which could be modified as necessary, to create a template for new cities and towns. I suspect that more than a few people among us might aspire to emulate the likes of Archias, Cadmus, and Dido.

Terraforming the Earth

Some people, such as Elon Musk, see terraforming another planet as a likely part of the human future. Frankly, the idea never captured my imagination. All the planets we know about are totally unsuited to human life: they're too hot or too cold, they have little or no atmosphere, or like Jupiter they're a swirling mass of lethal gases possibly surrounding a hot soup that may or may not have a solid core. Even Mars, the least implausible candidate for human habitation, looks wholly unwelcoming in the recent rover images. Earth is beautiful and everyone I know lives here. The idea of terraforming another planet is temptingly ambitious if we're looking for a big project to revive the frontier spirit. Still, I'm not quite there yet. Besides, there are large parts of our own planet that could use some terraforming, so to speak, to return them to a condition more supportive of long-term human habitation.

Human societies again and again have depleted resources they rely upon, or have otherwise made their environment uninhabitable. This does not mean that humans are a blight upon the earth—only that their ingenuity in making use of the earth's resources has often been applied without an understanding of long-term consequences. The first known large-scale instance of environmental degradation occurred in Mesopotamia four thousand years ago. The irrigation practices that had long been used for growing food crops on the dry plains increased the salinity of the soil to the point that crop yields dropped disastrously, leading to the decline of the Sumerian/Akkadian civilization. The seminomadic Amorites then became the leading power in Mesopotamia, adopting much of the old civilization and establishing a capital at Babylon, hundreds of miles upriver from the earlier centers. A new flowering of civilization began particularly under Hammurabi (ca. 1792–1750 BC).

In past eras, a whole society might pick up stakes and find a new place to settle. That's much harder now, though mass migrations still occur. The Dust Bowl of the 1930s prompted the exodus of about 2.5 million people out of the Great Plains. The underlying cause was decades of intensive farming of marginal land by settlers who didn't understand the region's ecology. When crops failed after several years of drought, the overplowed soil was exposed to wind storms. Federal programs were set up to encourage farming practices that protect topsoil, the thin, nutrient-dense layer that holds moisture, but the problem of soil degradation has not been solved. Another Dust Bowl event is not an impossibility.

Topsoil erosion is a global problem, and the basic reason for it has not changed since the Mesopotamian civilization thousands of years ago: People need a reliable source of food, so they use the methods that produce it most abundantly. Modern industrial farming practices have been very successful in providing abundant food. The Green Revolution of the 1950s and 1960s greatly increased the productivity of the land—by as much as forty times in some places—through the use of chemical fertilizers, pesticides, and newly created high-yield varieties of crops, particularly wheat, corn, and soy beans in the United States. A steady supply of plentiful food is a good thing in itself, but the methods employed to provide it have proved to be profoundly harmful in the long term.

"The modern combination of intensive tilling, lack of cover crops, synthetic fertilizers and pesticide use has left farmland stripped of the nutrients, minerals and microbes that support healthy plant life," notes an article in the *Guardian*.[16] Topsoil in the United States is believed to be eroding at ten times the rate it can be replaced. At least 75 percent of American agricultural land has been seriously degraded by erosion, which will lead to a crisis later this century unless there is a general shift to more sustainable farming practices, such as the no-till method that some farmers are now using. Overtilling lowers the capacity of the ground to hold water, leaving it more exposed to erosion and increasing atmospheric dust, which can reduce rainfall and lead to desertification.

The good news is that desertification can be reversed, and it's being done in small-scale projects around the world. China successfully undertook a very large restoration effort known as the Loess Plateau Watershed Rehabilitation Project. Begun in 1994, it has transformed more than 35,000 square kilometers of dusty, barren desert into a thriving, productive, beautiful place. For interested readers, I suggest searching "Loess Plateau before and after" on the internet. The images are striking.

A number of private rehabilitation projects have been launched in the United States, but they touch a minuscule fraction of the agricultural land. If a large producer changes practice, its business model will collapse under market competition unless the new practices become the norm. National leadership would be needed to make that happen.

Much has been learned about soil ecology since the advent of automated tilling machines and chemical fertilizers. We can use that knowledge to make the land more sustainably productive and also make food crops more nutritious from the complex composition of rehabilitated topsoil. The ground would better hold water, natural weather patterns would return, and aquifers in the American Midwest would be replenished. The droughts caused by topsoil erosion would be reduced or averted.

A large, long-term commitment to restoring America's agricultural lands to a healthier condition would bring a great and enduring benefit to the country. Upgrading the entire continent would be the largest infrastructure project in human history—like Elon's dream of terraforming but without the space travel. My modest proposal is this: let's terraform the American Midwest, and then we can discuss Mars.

Everyone has a theory of what's wrong with America. The sense of civilizational exhaustion is almost palpable. People have enough to eat—arguably too much. There's no sense of meaning. There is a growing feeling of entropy.

To regain national vitality, what we need most is a sense of shared purpose—something that the country does in which everyone has a role, big or small. Lacking such a purpose, we've too often idolized our processes, such as the way we choose our political leaders, rather than judging the quality of the leaders the process produces. But we can change this by focusing on clear, tangible goals and then getting to work. When people know what they're trying to achieve and work toward it together, subordinating parochial interests and rivalries to something bigger, a sense of comity and solidarity naturally forms between them. That's true whether we're building new cities or terraforming the Midwest.

As we move forward in a revitalizing project, the overall goals should include higher living standards, broadly shared prosperity, healthier people, longer lives, robust family formation, family stability, lower crime rates, more social trust, and greater trust in institutions. More specifically, here are four simple, measurable goals that should be at the heart of a revitalizing project:

1) A family wage. It should be possible to raise a family of four, own a home, and pay for education and health care on a single median wage. This was possible in America until the middle of the 1980s. It should be so again.

2) More children. At a minimum, the total fertility rate should be enough to sustain our existing population.

3) Less disease. Reduce the prevalence of the chronic inflammatory diseases that have skyrocketed in recent decades, with a huge cost in lives.

4) Longer lives. If Americans are healthier, they can live longer too.

These goals should form the nonnegotiable basis for evaluating every big project, including American politics itself.

How do we achieve these goals? Through science, decentralization, smaller institutions, lots of latitude for families, religion, space for innovation in governance, and room for visionaries to experiment. People must be able to think freely, speak freely, and try new ideas, some of which will be unorthodox, unsuccessful, dangerous, or just plain weird. And we must marry this to improvements in the real world.

We need to recapture the frontier mindset that pulled us forward as a nation for much of our history. A frontier is a challenging place full of unknown risks, a place where ingenuity and cooperation are necessary for survival. When the American frontier closed, we became more risk-averse as well as more fractious and self-interested. We can get our vitality back by opening new frontiers, if only metaphorical ones.

Napoleon famously said that what was most necessary for victory was audacity, always audacity. Getting to work on any of the projects described in this chapter would be audacious—but then so is America.

NOTES

Introduction

1   Julius Bellanco, "The Plumbing Census," *Plumbing and Mechanical* Magazine, June 1, 2010, https://www.pmmag.com/articles/93671-the-plumbing-census#:~:text=It%20has%20been%20estimated%20that,of%20homes%20with%20indoor%20plumbing.

Chapter 1: An Age of Decay

1   Los Angeles Metro Area Population 1950–2021, Macrotrends, https://www.macrotrends.net/cities/23052/los-angeles/population.

2   Tom O'Neill, *Chaos: Charles Manson, the CIA, and the Secret History of the Sixties* (Little, Brown & Co., 2019), p. 208.

3   J. D. Montagu, "Length of life in the ancient world: a controlled study," *Journal of the Royal Society of Medicine* 87 (January 1994): 25–26, https://www.ncbi.nlm.nih.gov/pmc/articles/PMC1294277/pdf/jrsocmed00089-0029.pdf.

4   Daniel E. Lieberman, "Active Grandparenting, Costly Repair," *Harvard Magazine*, September–October 2020, https://harvardmagazine.com/2020/09/features-active-grandparenting.

5   Sherryl L. Murphy et al., "Mortality in the United States, 2017," NCHS Data Brief No. 328, November 2018, Centers for Disease Control and Prevention, https://www.cdc.gov/nchs/products/databriefs/db328.htm#:~:text=Data%20from%20the%20National%20Vital,to%2078.6%20years%20in%202017.

6   Steven H. Woolf et al., "Effect of the covid-19 pandemic in 2020 on life

expectancy across populations in the USA and other high income countries: simulations of provisional mortality data," *BMJ* 2021;373:n1343 (June 24, 2021), https://www.bmj.com/content/373/bmj.n1343.

7   World Inequality Database, Top 10% national income share, https://wid. world/world/#sptinc_p90p100_z/US/last/eu/k/p/yearly/s/false/32.9755/60/ curve/false/country.

8   Austin Clemens, "Eight graphs that tell the story of U.S. economic inequality," Washington Center for Equitable Growth, December 19, 2019, https:// equitablegrowth.org/eight-graphs-that-tell-the-story-of-u-s-economic-inequality/.

9   Hugo Erken, Frank van Es, and Philip Marey, "Make American Productivity Great Again—Background report," *RaboResearch*, Rabobank, May 2, 2019, https://economics.rabobank.com/publications/2019/may/make-american-productivity-great-again--background-report/.

10 Tyler Cowen, *The Great Stagnation: How America Ate All the Low-Hanging Fruit of Modern History, Got Sick, and Will (Eventually) Feel Better* (Dutton, 2011), p. 24.

11 Amanda Fischer, "The rising financialization of the U.S. economy harms workers and their families, threatening a strong recovery," Washington Center for Equitable Growth, May 11, 2011, https://equitablegrowth.org/the-rising-financialization-of-the-u-s-economy-harms-workers-and-their-families-threatening-a-strong-recovery/.

12 Claire Bushey, "US airlines reveal profitability of frequent flyer programmes," *Financial Times*, September 15, 2020, https://www.ft.com/content/1bb94ed9-90de-4f15-aee0-3bf390b0f85e.

13 M. Blaug, *Economic Theory in Retrospect*, 4th ed. (Cambridge University Press, 1985).

14 Louis Rouanet, "How Central Banking Increased Inequality," *Mises Wire*, August 15, 2017, Mises Institute, https://mises.org/library/how-central-banking-increased-inequality.

15 Greg Robb, "Obama alumni shed light on why so little was done to aid homeowners in crisis," *Market Watch*, February 11, 2016, https://www.marketwatch.com/story/obama-alumni-shed-light-on-why-so-little-was-done-to-aid-homeowners-in-crisis-2016-02-11.

16 Kartikay Mehrotra and Laura J. Keller, "Wells Fargo's Fake Accounts Grow to 3.5 Million in Suit," *Bloomberg*, May 12, 2017, https://www.bloomberg.com/news/articles/2017-05-12/wells-fargo-bogus-account-estimate-in-suit-grows-to-3-5-million.

17 Trading Economics, "United States Households Debt to GDP," https://tradingeconomics.com/united-states/households-debt-to-gdp.

18   Statista, "Estimated median age of Americans at their first wedding in the United States from 1998 to 2019, by sex," January 20, 2021, https://www.statista.com/statistics/371933/median-age-of-us-americans-at-their-first-wedding/.

Chapter 2: Sensemaking, Hyperreality, and Frayed Consensus

1   Ron Marshall, "How Many Ads Do You See in One Day?" Red Crow Marketing, September 10, 2015, https://www.redcrowmarketing.com/2015/09/10/many-ads-see-one-day/; Amy Watson, "Media Use—Statistics & Facts," Statista, March 23, 2020, https://www.statista.com/topics/1536/media-use/.

2   Norman Davies, *Vanished Kingdoms: The Rise and Fall of States and Nations* (Penguin, 2012), p. 318.

3   Rep. Ro Khanna, quote given directly to me via text.

4   Ana Eiras and Brett Schaefer, "Argentina's Economic Crisis: An 'Absence of Capitalism,'" Heritage Foundation, Backgrounder #1432, April 19, 2001, https://web.archive.org/web/20120119174030/http://www.heritage.org/research/reports/2001/04/argentinas-economic-crisis-an-absence-of-capitalism.

5   GDP per capita (current US$)—Argentina, World Bank Data.

6   Chris Kahn, "On Trump's ties to Russia, Americans have made up their minds: Reuters/Ipsos poll," Reuters, March 8, 2019, https://www.reuters.com/article/us-usa-trump-russia-poll/on-trumps-ties-to-russia-americans-have-made-up-their-minds-reuters-ipsos-poll-idUSKCN1QP1E5.

7   Lynn Vavreck, "A Measure of Identity: Are You Wedded to Your Party?" *New York Times*, January 31, 2017, https://www.nytimes.com/2017/01/31/upshot/are-you-married-to-your-party.html.

8   Anthony Downs, *An Economic Theory of Democracy* (Harper, 1957), chap. 8.

9   I am, of course, aware of the existence of slavery during this period and how enslaved people were not free to decide if or how they would participate in the American project. That subject is well explored elsewhere by many other people.

Chapter 3: Institutional Betrayal and Elite Sociopathology

1   Jennifer J. Freyd, "Institutional Betrayal and Institutional Courage," University of Oregon, https://dynamic.uoregon.edu/jjf/institutionalbetrayal/#:~:text=The%20term%20institutional%20betrayal%20refers,the%20context%20of%20the%20institution.

2   "Message-relay systems of the ancient world," *Britannica*, https://www.britannica.com/topic/postal-system/History#ref367055.

3   Sir James Goldsmith, *The Trap* (Carroll & Graf, 1994), p. 16.

4   Eric Weinstein, *The Portal* podcast, episode 30 (April 16, 2020), transcript at https://moses.land/transcript-ross-douthat-and-eric-weinstein-on-the-portal-episode-30/.

5   HRC Paid Speeches, email dated January 25, 2016, released by WikiLeaks, https://wikileaks.org/podesta-emails/emailid/927.

6   Felix Richter, "Amazon Challenges Ad Duopoly," Statista, February 1, 2019, https://www.statista.com/chart/17109/us-digital-advertising-market-share/.

7   Megan Graham, "Amazon is eating into Google's most important business: Search advertising," CNBC, October 15, 2019, https://www.cnbc.com/2019/10/15/amazon-is-eating-into-googles-dominance-in-search-ads.html.

8   Matthew Zeitlin, "Why WeWork Went Wrong," *Guardian*, December 20, 2019, https://www.theguardian.com/business/2019/dec/20/why-wework-went-wrong.

9   Reeves Wiedeman, "The I in We: How did WeWork's Adam Neumann turn office space with 'community' into a $47 billion company? Not by sharing," *New York Intelligencer*, June 10, 2019, https://nymag.com/intelligencer/2019/06/wework-adam-neumann.html.

10   "Big corporate's quest to be hip is helping WeWork," *Economist*, July 14, 2018, https://www.economist.com/business/2018/07/12/big-corporates-quest-to-be-hip-is-helping-wework.

11   Wiedeman, "The I in We."

12   Leslie Picker and Deirdre Bosa, "WeWork doesn't have a single woman director, according to IPO filing," CNBC, August 14, 2019, updated August 15, 2019, https://www.cnbc.com/2019/08/14/wework-doesnt-have-a-single-woman-director-according-to-ipo-filing.html.

13   Maureen Farrell and Eliot Brown, "SoftBank to Boost Stake in WeWork in Deal That Cuts Most Ties With Neumann," *Wall Street Journal*, October 22, 2019, https://www.wsj.com/articles/softbank-to-take-control-of-wework-11571746483?mod=e2tw.

14   Mark J. Perry, "Chart of the day: Administrative bloat in US public schools," American Enterprise Institute, March 9, 2013, https://www.aei.org/carpe-diem/chart-of-the-day-administrative-bloat-in-us-public-schools/.

15   Monya Baker, "1,500 scientists lift the lid on reproducibility," *Nature*, May 25, 2016, https://www.nature.com/news/1-500-scientists-lift-the-lid-on-reproducibility-1.19970.

16   "The Replication Crisis: Flaws in Mainstream Science," 2013 discussion, Gwern.net, https://www.gwern.net/Replication.

17   Simona Warrella, "Feeling of loneliness among adults 2021, by country,"

Statista, March 19, 2021, https://www.statista.com/statistics/1222815/loneliness-among-adults-by-country/.

18 Centers for Disease Contol and Prevention, "Loneliness and Social Isolation Linked to Serious Health Conditions," https://www.cdc.gov/aging/publications/features/lonely-older-adults.html#:~:text=A%20report%20from%20the%20National,considered%20to%20be%20socially%20isolated.

Chapter 4: The Politics of Decay

1 Michael Lind, "The New Class War," *American Affairs* 1:2 (Summer 2017), https://americanaffairsjournal.org/2017/05/new-class-war/.

2 For a fascinating account of the Tate-LaBianca murders—far better than Vincent Bugliosi's questionable account—see Tom O'Neill, *Chaos: Charles Manson, the CIA, and the Secret History of the Sixties* (Little, Brown & Co., 2019).

3 Bureau of Labor Statistics, "U.S. Weekly Earnings of Wage and Salary Workers, First Quarter 2020," News Release, U.S. Department of Labor, April 16, 2021, https://www.bls.gov/news.release/pdf/wkyeng.pdf.

4 Richard W. Reeves and Eleanor Krause, "Raj Chetty in 14 charts: Big findings on opportunity and mobility we should all know," Brookings, January 11, 2018, https://www.brookings.edu/blog/social-mobility-memos/2018/01/11/raj-chetty-in-14-charts-big-findings-on-opportunity-and-mobility-we-should-know/.

5 Raj Chetty et al., "The Fading American Dream: Declining Mobility and Increasing Inequality," *Evonomics*, April 27, 2017, https://evonomics.com/the-end-of-upward-mobility-america-concentrated-wealth-chetty/.

6 Congressional Research Service, *Real Wage Trends, 1979 to 2019*, updated December 28, 2020, https://fas.org/sgp/crs/misc/R45090.pdf.

7 Alana Benson, "Here are the average retirement savings by age: Is it enough?" *Market Watch*, December 6, 2020, https://www.marketwatch.com/story/here-are-the-average-retirement-savings-by-age-is-it-enough-2020-11-16.

8 Statista, "Percentage of the U.S. population with a college degree, by gender 1940–2019," https://www.statista.com/statistics/184272/educational-attainment-of-college-diploma-or-higher-by-gender/.

9 Andrea Koncz, "Salary Trends Through Salary Survey: A Historical Perspective on Starting Salaries for New College Graduates," NACE, August 2, 2016, https://www.naceweb.org/job-market/compensation/salary-trends-through-salary-survey-a-historical-perspective-on-starting-salaries-for-new-college-graduates/.

10 Tuition data from Statista, "Average annual charges per student for higher education in public and private institutions in the United States from 1970 to

2019," https://www.statista.com/statistics/203056/average-annual-charges-for-higher-education-in-the-us/. An inflation factor of 6.71 was used for the period 1970–2018.

11 Data from the U.S. Federal Reserve and the Federal Reserve Bank of New York analyzed by Student Loan Hero, "A Look at the Shocking Student Loan Debt Statistics for 2021," updated January 27, 2021, https://studentloanhero.com/student-loan-debt-statistics/.

12 American Bar Association, "Historical Trend in Total National Lawyer Population, 1878–2021," ABA National Lawyer Population Survey, https://www.americanbar.org/content/dam/aba/administrative/market_research/total-national-lawyer-population-1878-2022.pdf.

13 Quoted in Peter Turchin, *War and Peace and War: The Rise and Fall of Empires* (Plume, 2007), p. 277.

14 Turchin, *War and Peace and War*, pp. 277–78.

15 Aris Roussinos, "The Tories against democracy," *UnHerd*, https://unherd.com/2020/11/the-tories-against-democracy/, quoting from William Sanderson, *Statecraft: A Treatise on the Concerns of Our Sovereign Lord the King* (1932).

Chapter 5: America in the World

1 Lionel Barber, Henry Foy, and Alex Barker, "Vladimir Putin says liberalism has 'become obsolete,'" *Financial Times*, June 27, 2019, https://www.ft.com/content/670039ec-98f3-11e9-9573-ee5cbb98ed36.

2 Ivan Watson, Maria Stromova, and Antonia Mortensen, "The rise of the Russian Orthodox Church," CNN, March 30, 2017, https://www.cnn.com/2017/03/30/europe/russian-orthodox-church-resurgence/index.html.

3 Ibid.

4 Quoted in Aris Roussinos, "The irresistible rise of the civilisation-state," *UnHerd*, August 6, 2020, https://unherd.com/2020/08/the-irresistible-rise-of-the-civilisation-state/. I heartily recommend this excellent essay for a fuller treatment of the subject. Some of the other quotes in this section also come from Roussinos, who pointed me to some sources of which I had not been aware. I have also drawn on the work of many other people, including Samuel Huntington and Bruno Macaes, to form an understanding of the rising civilization-states.

5 Zhang Weiwei, *The China Wave: Rise of a Civilizational State* (World Century Publishing Corp., 2012), p. 55.

6 Ibid., p. 66.

7 Chris Buckley, "'Clean Up This Mess': The Chinese Thinkers Behind Xi's Hard Line," *New York Times*, August 2, 2020, updated August 12, 2020, https://www.

nytimes.com/2020/08/02/world/asia/china-hong-kong-national-security-law.
html.

8   Jiang Shigong, "Empire and World Order," Introduction and Translation by
    David Ownby, Reading the China Dream, https://www.readingthechinadream.
    com/jiang-shigong-empire-and-world-order.html.

9   Ambassadors' conference—Speech by M. Emmanuel Macron, President of the
    Republic, August 17, 2019, Francija Latvijā, Ambassade de France en Lettonie,
    https://lv.ambafrance.org/Ambassadors-conference-Speech-by-M-Emmanuel-
    Macron-President-of-the-Republic.

10 Ibid.

11 Xi Jinping, *The Governance of China* (Beijing: Foreign Language Press, 2014,
    2018).

12 Tanner Greer, "The Theory of History That Guides Xi Jinping," *Palladium*,
    July 8, 2020, https://palladiummag.com/2020/07/08/the-theory-of-history-
    that-guides-xi-jinping/; and Timothy Heath, "The 'Holistic Security Concept':
    The Securitization of Policy and Increasing Risk of Militarized Crisis," *China
    Brief* 15:12 (June 19, 2015), Jamestown Foundation, https://jamestown.
    org/program/the-holistic-security-concept-the-securitization-of-policy-and-
    increasing-risk-of-militarized-crisis/.

13 Manfred Weber, @ManfredWeber, Twitter, December 30, 2020, https://
    twitter.com/ManfredWeber/status/1344205681071693824?s=20.

14 Chatham House, "Does COVID-19 Spell the End of America's Interest in
    Globalization?" May 22, 2020, https://youtu.be/oiK702386i8.

15 Roussinos, "The irresistible rise of the civilisation-state."

Chapter 6: Golden Ages and the Roots of Vitality

1   A. Trevor Hodge, *The Woodwork of Greek Roofs* (Cambridge University Press,
    1960), p. 41.

2   John Munro, "Medieval Population Dynamics to 1500, Part C: the major
    population changes and demographic trends from 1250 to ca. 1520,"
    Department of Economics, University of Toronto, https://www.economics.
    utoronto.ca/munro5/L02MedievalPopulationC.pdf.

3   "The Industrial Revolution / Manchester," http://www.woodville.org/
    documentos/130802the-industrial-revolution-manchester.pdf.

4   Eric Hopkins, *Industrialisation and Society: A Social History, 1830–1951*
    (Routledge, 2000), p. 2.

5   Nicholas T. Phillipson, *David Hume: The Philosopher as Historian* (Yale
    University Press, 2012), p. 32.

6   Francis Fukuyama, *The End of History and the Last Man* (Free Press, 2006), p. 315.

7   George Frederick Zook, *Report of the Commission for an Investigation Relative to Opportunities and Methods for Technical and Higher Education in the Commonwealth Appointed Under Authority of Chapter 33 of the Resolves of 1922, including Report of a Fact-finding Survey of Technical and Higher Education in Massachusetts* (1924), p. 51.

8   "The Curse of Credentialism," *NYU Dispatch*, November 17, 2017, https://wp.nyu.edu/dispatch/2017/11/17/the-curse-of-credentialism/.

9   Sam Levin, "'Facebook told advertisers it can identify teens feeling 'insecure' and 'worthless,' " *Guardian*, May 1, 2017, https://www.theguardian.com/technology/2017/may/01/facebook-advertising-data-insecure-teens.

10 Holly B. Shakya and Nicholas A. Christakis, "A New, More Rigorous Study Confirms: The More You Use Facebook, the Worse You Feel," *Harvard Business Review*, April 10, 2017, https://hbr.org/2017/04/a-new-more-rigorous-study-confirms-the-more-you-use-facebook-the-worse-you-feel.

11 Charter Cities Institute, "An Introduction to Charter Cities," https://www.chartercitiesinstitute.org/intro.

12 Nell Frizzell, "Is Having A Baby In 2021 Pure Environmental Vandalism?" *Vogue* (UK), April 25, 2021, https://www.vogue.co.uk/mini-vogue/article/having-a-child-sustainable.

13 Travis Rieder, "Science proves kids are bad for Earth. Morality suggests we stop having them," NBC News, Opinion, November 15, 2017, https://www.nbcnews.com/think/opinion/science-proves-kids-are-bad-earth-morality-suggests-we-stop-ncna820781.

14 Tyler Cowen, "My Conversation with Matt Yglesias," *Marginal Revolution*, September 9, 2020, https://marginalrevolution.com/marginalrevolution/2020/09/my-conversation-with-matt-yglesias.html.

15 Rieder, "Science proves kids are bad for Earth.

Chapter 7: Big Country, Big Projects

1   Elon Musk, @elonmusk, Twitter, January 14, 2021, https://twitter.com/elonmusk/status/1349977642708168704?s=20.

2   I want to give credit to a few people whose writing has pointed me toward some of the technologies mentioned in this chapter, specifically Eli Dourado, Balaji Srinivasan, and Peter Thiel.

3   Jeff Nobbs, "The World Needs an Oil Change," Zero Acre, February 2, 2022, https://www.zeroacre.com/blog/the-world-needs-an-oil-change; Centers for Disease Control and Prevention, "Chronic Diseases in America," https://www.cdc.gov/chronicdisease/resources/infographic/chronic-diseases.htm; World Health Organization, "The Global Strategy on Diet, Physical Activity and Health," https://www.who.int/dietphysicalactivity/media/en/gsfs_general.pdf;

George Weisz, "EPIDEMIOLOGY and Health Care Reform: The National Health Survey of 1935–1936," *American Journal of Public Health*, March 2011, https://www.ncbi.nlm.nih.gov/pmc/articles/PMC3036678/.

4   Nobbs, "The World Needs an Oil Change."

5   MedlinePlus, "What are genome editing and CRISPR-Cas9?" https://medlineplus.gov/genetics/understanding/genomicresearch/genomeediting/.

6   NCI Staff, "How CRISPR Is Changing Cancer Research and Treatment," National Cancer Institute, July 27, 2020, https://www.cancer.gov/news-events/cancer-currents-blog/2020/crispr-cancer-research-treatment.

7   Eli Dourado, "Notes on technology in the 2020s," blog post, December 31, 2020, https://elidourado.com/blog/notes-on-technology-2020s/.

8   Ibid.

9   Natalie G. Adams et al., "Regulating the 'Schooled' Body," Section 2 in *Learning to Teach: A Critical Approach to Field Experiences* (Taylor & Frances, 2006), https://www.google.com/books/edition/Learning_to_Teach/tqOPAgAAQBAJ?hl=en&gbpv=0.

10   Peter Coy, "Demanding a Bachelor's Degree for a Middle-Skill Job Is Just Plain Dumb," *Bloomberg*, October 25, 2017, https://www.bloomberg.com/news/articles/2017-10-25/demanding-a-bachelor-s-degree-for-a-middle-skill-job-is-just-plain-dumb.

11   Vitalik Buterin, "The Meaning of Decentralization," Medium, February 6, 2017, https://medium.com/@VitalikButerin/the-meaning-of-decentralization-a0c92b76a274.

12   Balaji Srinivasan, @balajis, Twitter, August 3, 2020, https://twitter.com/balajis/status/1290326486382022656?s=20.

13   Charter Cities Institute, "An Introduction to Charter Cities," https://www.chartercitiesinstitute.org/intro.

14   Jeffrey Mason, "An Analysis of Nevada's Proposed Innovation Zones Law," Charter Cities Institute, February 5, 2021, https://www.chartercitiesinstitute.org/post/an-analysis-of-nevadas-proposed-innovation-zones-law.

15   Ibid.

16   Susan Crosier, "The world needs topsoil to grow 95% of its food—but it's rapidly disappearing," *Guardian*, May 30, 2019, https://www.theguardian.com/us-news/2019/may/30/topsoil-farming-agriculture-food-toxic-america; and Richard Schiffman, "Why It's Time to Stop Punishing Our Soils with Fertilizers," *E360*, May 3, 2017, Yale School of the Environment, https://e360.yale.edu/features/why-its-time-to-stop-punishing-our-soils-with-fertilizers-and-chemicals.

INDEX

network effects, 107–9
Neumann, Adam, 47–48, 50–51
Neumann, Rebekah, 47
Nevada: Innovation Zones, 138–39
New Deal, 63
Nicaragua, 90
Nobel Prize, 106
Normans, 39
North American Free Trade Agreement
    (NAFTA), 42
Noyce, Robert, 100
nuclear power, xviii, 120, 121
Nunn, Sam, 46

Obolensky, Dimitri, 25
Oculus, 102
oligarchy, 36, 63–64
Oneida Community, 111
O'Neill, Tom, 2
Opportunity Zones, 138
Oracle, 100
OxyContin, 53

Packard, David, 101, 102
Paleo Manifesto, The (Durant), 124
Palladio, Andrea, 106
Palo Alto Research Center (PARC),
    100, 101
Parsons, Jack, 1–2
PayPal, 100
peasant rebellions, 73–74
Peat, Ray, 124–25
Peloponnesian War, 89, 95
Pelosi, Nancy, 29
penicillin, xiii
Perry, William, 46
Pew, J. Edgar, 40
Pew Research Center, 32, 33
Pfizer, xiii, 53
pharmaceutical industry, 123–24
Philip the Arab (emperor), 38
physics, xiii
Plato, 42–43
Playfair, John, 99

Pliny the Elder, 5
Ponzi, Charles, 48
population growth, xii, xvii, 1, 10, 98
Pre-Raphaelite Brotherhood, 110
Princeton University, 104
productivity, xvii–xviii, xx, 19, 30;
    agricultural, 10–11, 98; and
    innovation, 10–12, 39–41, 59, 98,
    103, 119–20
Progressive Era, 63, 111; and World War
    I, xx
Purdue Pharmaceutical, 53
Putin, Vladimir, 36, 83, 84–85
Putnam, Robert, xv

railroads, 60, 98; transcontinental, xii
Ratajkowski, Emily, 49
Reagan, Ronald, xvii
Reece, Florence, 40
religion, xi, 32, 34, 88; communities
    of, 111, 112; and family, 113;
    monuments of, 24, 113; in Russia,
    84–85; as unifying, 24–26, 113–14;
    see also Christianity
Republican Party, 43, 78–79
resource curse, xxii; and reserve
    currency, 16–17
Revolutions of 1848, 58
Richelieu, Cardinal (Armand-Jean du-
    Plessis), 66–67, 74
Rockefeller, John D., xiii
Rogers, William Barton, 104–5, 106, 110
Roman Catholic Church, 113–14
Rome (ancient), xi; Augustan era, 37–
    38, 56; barracks emperors in, 38–39,
    56; decentralized governance in, 133;
    Lycurgus cup, x; Pax Romana, 37;
    religion in, 25
Rubin, Robert, 44, 79
Ruskin, John, 110–11
Russell, Austin, 129
Russia, xxii, 83; attack on Ukraine, 85;
    as civilization-state, 84–85; oligarchs
    in, 36